Wood Pellet Grill & Smoker Cookbook:

The Ultimate Recipes for Perfect Smoking

Thomas Beard

© Copyright 2019 by Thomas Beard
All rights reserved.
This document is geared towards providing exact and reliable information with regards to the topic and issue covered. The publication is sold with the idea that the publisher is not required to render accounting, officially permitted, or otherwise, qualified services. If advice is necessary, legal or professional, a practiced individual in the profession should be ordered.

- From a Declaration of Principles which was accepted and approved equally by a Committee of the American Bar Association and a Committee of Publishers and Associations.

In no way is it legal to reproduce, duplicate, or transmit any part of this document in either electronic means or in printed format. Recording of this publication is strictly prohibited and any storage of this document is not allowed unless with written permission from the publisher. All rights reserved.

The information provided herein is stated to be truthful and consistent, in that any liability, in terms of inattention or otherwise, by any usage or abuse of any policies, processes, or directions contained within is the solitary and utter responsibility of the recipient reader. Under no circumstances will any legal responsibility or blame be held against the publisher for any reparation, damages, or monetary loss due to the information herein, either directly or indirectly.

Respective authors own all copyrights not held by the publisher.

The information herein is offered for informational purposes solely, and is universal as so. The presentation of the information is without contract or any type of guarantee assurance. The trademarks that are used are without any consent, and the publication of the trademark is without permission or backing by the trademark owner. All trademarks and brands within this book are for clarifying purposes only and are the owned by the owners themselves, not affiliated with this document.

Abbreviations

Gram	=	g
Milligram	=	mg
Ounce	=	oz
Pound	=	lb
Tablespoon	=	tbsp
Teaspoon	=	tsp

Note:

- **The nutritional facts for each recipe are a summation of the nutritional facts of each ingredient included in the recipe.**

Table of Contents

Introduction 1
    Chapter One 3
        Beef and Lamb Recipes 3
Pellet Grill Meatloaf 3
BBQ Brisket 6
Tri tip Roast 9
Baby Back Rib 12
Beef Jerky 15
Beef Skewers 18
Smoked Italian Meatballs 21
Prime Rib Roast 24
Beef Tenderloin 28
Beef Stuffed Bell Pepper 31
Braised Beef Short ribs 34
Grilled Filet Mignon 38
Hickory Rack of Lamb 40
Leg of Lamb 44
BBQ Burnt Ends 47
Smoked Pulled Beef 51
Beef Chili 54
Stuffed Flank Steak 58
Beef Bourguignon 61
Beef Stew 66
    Chapter Two 70
        Poultry Recipes 70

Beef Can Smoked Chicken 70

Marinated Smoked Turkey Breast 73

Maple Bourbon Turkey 76

Huli Huli Chicken 80

Herb Smoked Chicken 83

Honey Sesame Chicken Wings 86

Cornish Game Hen 88

BBQ Pulled Chicken 92

Smoked Chicken Drumsticks 95

Chicken Cordon Bleu 98

Smoked Whole Duck 102

Chicken Tenders 105

Thanksgiving Turkey 108

Spatchcock Smoked Turkey 111

Smoked Chicken Leg Quarters 114

Chicken Fajitas 117

Grilled Chicken Kebabs 120

Chicken Enchiladas 123

Hoisin Turkey Wings 126

Turkey Jerky 130

Honey Baked Mustard Chicken 133

Chicken Nuggets 137

    Chapter Three 141

        Pork Recipes 141

Pork Burnt Ends 141

Pork Prime Rib 145

Grilled Carnitas 148

Stuffed Tenderloin 151

Pork Kebabs 153

Scotch Eggs 158

Maplewood Bourbon BBQ Ham 161

Country Style Pork Ribs 164

Pork Chops 167

Smoked Pulled Pork 171

Porchetta 175

Pork Jerky 179

   Chapter Four 183

      Seafood Recipes 183

Grilled Lobster Tail 183

Halibut 186

Grilled Salmon 189

BBQ Shrimp 192

Grilled Tuna 195

Oyster in Shell 198

Grilled King Crab Legs 201

Cajun Smoked Catfish 204

Smoked Scallops 207

Grilled Tilapia 210

Shrimp Scampi 213

Smoked Shrimp 216

   Chapter Five 220

      Wild Meat Recipes 220

Goat Chops 220

Smoked Goose Breast 223

Smoked Venison Tenderloin 226

Smoked Rabbit 229

Spatchcock Smoked Quail 232

Smoked Pheasant 235

Rabbit Stew 238

Grilled Antelope 241

Elk Kebabs 244

Wild Boar 247

    Chapter Six 251

        Other Recipes 251

Roasted Chickpeas Snacks 251

Glazed Carrots 254

Simple Roasted Butternut Squash 257

Spiced Nuts 260

Grilled Potatoes 263

Eggplant Stuffed Lasagna 266

Chicken Quesadilla 270

Buffalo Chicken Meatballs 274

Cauliflower Hash Browns 277

Smoked Carrot Fries 280

Empanadas 283

Mango Bread 287

Kid-friendly Zucchini Bread 290

Grill Baked Shrimp 293

Mozzarella Meatballs 296

BBQ Pork Rinds 299

Chicken Parmesan 301

Beef and Bacon Casserole 304

Keto Quiche 308

Breakfast Sausage Casserole 311

Crunchy Avocado Fries 314

Low Carb Almond Flour Bread 317

Rosemary Cheese Breadstick 320

Cinnamon Almond Shortbread 323

Introduction

Why smoking?
I guess the first question we need to ask ourselves here is "why smoking". The biggest answer for this question is FLAVOR. There are different ways of cooking; however, when it comes to flavor, I consider smoking the big boss in the culinary world. I guess that is why people go to the extent of adding liquid smoke to their food even when they are not cooking on a smoker. Everyone seems tom like that natural smoke flavor that comes with smoked foods.
Smoking also gives your food a special aroma. When you smoke your food on the smoker, the fume of the wood used for smoking gives the food a mouthwatering flavor and aroma. Hardwoods such hickory, mesquite, maple, pecan, apple, alder and cherry have a way of taking your foods to another level of savory aroma.
Aside the fact that smoking adds more flavor and aroma to your food, smoking is a good way of preserving your food. I guess it is no longer a news that Smoked foods last longer, without losing much taste. Smoking reduces the moisture

content of your food, thus making it hard for bacteria to survive on the food. Smoking is a confirmed food preservation method that is cheap and efficient.

Smoking is quite fun. However, it is not everyone who knows how to smoke. This book is written to provide easy and flavorful wood pellet grill recipes with clear and simple instructions. It is cool to have a grill but it is cooler to know how to smoke different kinds of food with different techniques with the grill. This book feature 100 finger licking wood pellet grill recipes that will turn you to a guru in no time. Just get your grill and let's smoke something delicious. Enjoy!!!

Chapter One

Beef and Lamb Recipes

Pellet Grill Meatloaf

PREP TIME: 15 minutes
COOK TIME: 2 hour 30 minutes
SERVINGS: 8
Ingredients:
- 1 cup breadcrumbs
- 2 pounds ground beef
- ¼ pound ground sausage

- 2 large eggs (beaten)
- 2 garlic cloves (grated)
- ½ tsp ground black pepper
- ¼ tsp red pepper flakes
- ½ tsp salt or to taste
- 1 tsp dried parsley
- 1 green onion (chopped)
- 1 tsp paprika
- ½ tsp Italian seasoning
- 1 small onion (chopped)
- 1 cup milk
- 1 cup BBQ sauce
- ½ cup apple juice

Directions:
1. Preheat the grill to 225°F with lid closed for 15 minutes, using apple pellet
2. In a large mixing bowl, combine the egg, milk, parsley, onion, green onion, paprika, Italian seasoning, breadcrumbs, ground beef, ground sausage, salt, pepper flakes, black pepper and garlic. Mix thoroughly until the ingredients are well combined.
3. Form the mixture into a loaf and wrap the loaf loosely in tin foil and use a knife to poke some holes in the foil. The holes will allow smoke flavor to enter the loaf.

4. Place the wrapped loaf on the grill grate and grill for 1 hour 30 minutes.
5. Meanwhile, combine the BBQ sauce and apple juice in a mixing bowl.
6. Tear off the top half of the tin foil to apply the glaze. Apply the glaze over the meatloaf. Continue grilling until the internal temperature of the meatloaf is 160°F.
7. Remove the meatloaf from the grill and let it sit for a few minutes to cool.
8. Cut and serve.

Nutrition Facts

Servings: 8

Amount per serving

Calories 407

% Daily Value*

Total Fat 13.9g	18%
Saturated Fat 4.9g	25%
Cholesterol 162mg	54%
Sodium 810mg	35%
Total Carbohydrate 25.9g	9%
Dietary Fiber 1.3g	4%
Total Sugars 12.4g	
Protein 41.8g	

Nutrition Facts
Servings: 8

Vitamin D 5mcg	23%
Calcium 82mg	6%
Iron 23mg	126%
Potassium 671mg	14%

BBQ Brisket

PREP TIME: 20 minutes

COOK TIME: 10 hours
SERVINGS: 12
Ingredients:
- 1 (12-14) packer beef brisket
- 1 tsp cayenne pepper
- 1 tsp cumin
- 2 tbsp paprika
- 1 tbsp smoked paprika
- 1 tbsp onion powder
- 1/2 tbsp maple sugar
- 2 tsp ground black pepper
- 2 tsp kosher salt

Directions:
1. Combine all the ingredients except the brisket in a mixing bowl.
2. Season all sides of the brisket with the seasoning mixture as needed and wrap the brisket in a plastic wrap. Refrigerate for 12 hours or more.
3. Unwrap the brisket and let it sit for about 2 hours or until the brisket is at room temperature.
4. Preheat the pellet grill to 225°F with lid close, using mesquite or oak wood pellet.
5. Place the brisket on the grill grate and grill for about 6 hours. Remove the brisket from the grill and wrap with foil.

6. Return brisket to the grill and cook for about 4 hours or until the brisket's temperature reaches 204°F.
7. Remove the brisket from the grill and let it sit for about 40 minutes to cool.
8. Unwrap the brisket and cut into slices.

Nutrition Facts

Servings: 12

Amount per serving

Calories 992

% Daily Value*

Total Fat 33.2g	**43%**
Saturated Fat 12.5g	**62%**
Cholesterol 473mg	**158%**
Sodium 737mg	**32%**
Total Carbohydrate 1.9g	**1%**
Dietary Fiber 0.6g	**2%**
Total Sugars 0.7g	
Protein 160.9g	
Vitamin D 0mcg	0%
Calcium 14mg	1%
Iron 100mg	556%
Potassium 2176mg	

Tri tip Roast

PREP TIME: 10 minutes
COOK TIME: 1 hour 10 minutes
SERVINGS: 4
Ingredients:
- 2 pounds tri tip roast (silver skin and fat cap removed)
- 1 tsp salt
- 1 tsp ground black pepper
- ½ tsp paprika
- 1 tsp fresh rosemary
- 1 tsp garlic powder

- 1 tbsp olive oil

Directions:
1. Combine salt, pepper, garlic, paprika and rosemary.
2. Brush the tri tip generously with olive oil. Season the roast with seasoning mixture generously.
3. Preheat the grill smoker 225°F with lid closed for 15 minutes, using a hickory, mesquite or oak wood pellet.
4. Place the tri tip roast on the grill grate directly and cook for about 1 hour or until the tri tip's temperature reaches 135°F.
5. Remove the tri tip from the grill and wrap it with heavy duty foil. Set aside in a cooler.
6. Adjust the grill temperature to high and preheat with lid closed for 15 minutes.
7. Remove the tri tip from the foil and place it on the grill cook for 8 minutes, turning the tri tip after the first 4 minutes.
8. Remove the tri tip from the grill and let it rest for a few minutes to cool.
9. Cut the into slices against the grain and serve.

Nutrition Facts

Servings: 4

Amount per serving

Calories   448

	% Daily Value*
Total Fat 22.5g	29%
Saturated Fat 7.6g	38%
Cholesterol 161mg	54%
Sodium 707mg	31%
Total Carbohydrate 1.2g	0%
Dietary Fiber 0.4g	2%
Total Sugars 0.2g	
Protein 60.9g	
Vitamin D 0mcg	0%
Calcium 46mg	4%
Iron 4mg	23%
Potassium 795mg	17%

Baby Back Rib

PREP TIME: 15 minutes
COOK TIME: 5 hour 30 minutes
SERVINGS: 3
Ingredients:
- ½ cup BBQ sauce
- 1 rack baby back ribs
- 1 cup apple cider
- 1 tbsp Worcestershire sauce
- 1 tsp paprika
- ½ cup packed dark brown sugar
- 2 tbsp yellow mustard
- 2 tbsp honey
- 2 tbsp BBQ rub

Directions:
1. Remove the membrane on the back of the rib with a butter knife.
2. Combine the mustard, paprika, ½ cup apple cider and Worcestershire sauce.
3. Rub the mixture over the rib and season the rib with BBQ rub.
4. Start your grill on smoke setting and leave the lid opened until the fire starts.
5. Close the lid and preheat the grill to 180°F using hickory wood pellet.
6. Place the rib on the grill, smoke side up. Smoke for 3 hours.
7. Remove the ribs from the grill.
8. Tear off two large piece of heavy-duty aluminum foil and place one on a large working surface. Place the rib on the foil, rib side up.
9. Sprinkle the sugar over the rib. Top it with honey and the remaining apple cider.
10. Place the other piece of foil over the rib and crimp the edges of the aluminum foil pieces together to form an airtight seal.
11. Place the sealed rib on the grill and cook for 2 hours.
12. After the cooking cycle, gently remove the foil from the rib and discard it.

13. Brush all sides of the baby back rib with the BBQ sauce.
14. Return the rib to the grill grate directly and cook for an additional 30 minutes or until the sauce coating is firm and thick.
15. Remove the rib from the grill and let it cool for a few minutes.
16. Cut into sizes and serve.

Nutrition Facts

Servings: 3

Amount per serving

Calories 641

% Daily Value*

Total Fat 25.4g	33%
Saturated Fat 8.4g	42%
Cholesterol 0mg	0%
Sodium 2503mg	109%
Total Carbohydrate 71.6g	26%
Dietary Fiber 1g	3%
Total Sugars 64.5g	
Protein 0.7g	
Vitamin D 0mcg	0%
Calcium 19mg	1%

Nutrition Facts
Servings: 3

Iron 1mg	4%
Potassium 223mg	5%

Beef Jerky

PREP TIME: 15 minutes
COOK TIME: 5 hours
SERVINGS: 10
Ingredients:
Marinade:
- 1 cup pineapple juice

- ½ cup brown sugar
- 2 tbsp sriracha
- 2 tsp onion powder
- 2 tbsp minced garlic
- 2 tbsp rice wine vinegar
- 2 tbsp hoison
- 1 tsp salt
- 1 tbsp red pepper flakes
- 1 tbsp coarsely ground black pepper
- 2 cups coconut aminos
- 2 jalapenos (thinly sliced)

Meat:
- 3 pounds trimmed sirloin steak (sliced to ¼ inch thick)

Directions:
1. Combine all the marinade ingredients in a mixing bowl and mix until the ingredients are well combined.
2. Put the sliced sirloin in a gallon sized zip-lock bag and pour the marinade into the bag. Massage the marinade into the beef. Seal the bag and refrigerate for 8 hours.
3. Remove the zip-lock bag from the refrigerator.

4. Activate the pellet grill smoker setting and leave lip opened for 5 minutes until fire starts.
5. Close the lid and preheat your pellet grill to 180°F, using hickory pellet.
6. Remove the beef slices from the marinade and pat them dry with a paper towel.
7. Arrange the beef slice on the grill in a single layer. Smoke the beef for about 4 to 5 hours, turning often after the first 2 hours of smoking. The jerky should be dark and dry when it is done.
8. Remove the jerky from the grill and let it sit for about 1 hour to cool.
9. Serve immediately or store in airtight container and refrigerate for future use.

Nutrition Facts

Servings: 10

Amount per serving

Calories 365

% Daily Value*

Total Fat 8.9g	11%
Saturated Fat 3.2g	16%
Cholesterol 122mg	41%
Sodium 487mg	21%

Nutrition Facts
Servings: 10

Total Carbohydrate 24g	**9%**
Dietary Fiber 0.5g	**2%**
Total Sugars 11.5g	
Protein 41.8g	
Vitamin D 0mcg	0%
Calcium 25mg	2%
Iron 26mg	147%
Potassium 618mg	13%

Beef Skewers

PREP TIME: 15 minutes
COOK TIME: 8 minutes

SERVINGS: 8

Ingredients:
- 2 tbsp olive oil
- 2 pounds top round steak (cut to ¼-inch-thick and 2-inch-wide slices)
- 2 garlic cloves (finely chopped)
- ¼ cup water
- ½ cup soy sauce
- ¾ cup brown sugar
- 1 tbsp minced fresh ginger
- 1 tsp freshly ground black pepper or more to taste
- 3 tbsp red wine vinegar
- 3 tbsp dried basil
- Wooden or bamboo skewers (soaked in water for 30 minutes, at least)

Directions:
1. In a mixing bowl, combine the olive oil, sugar, ginger, garlic, sot sauce, water, vinegar, pepper and basil. Mix until the ingredients are well combined.
2. Pour the marinade into a zip-lock bag and add the steak slices. Massage the marinade into the steak slices. Refrigerate for 12 hours or more.

3. Remove the steak slices from the marinade and pat them dry with paper towel.
4. Thread the steak slices on to the soaked skewers.
5. Activate the smoke setting on your wood smoker grill, using a hickory wood pellet. Leave the lid opened until the fire is established.
6. Close the lid and preheat grill to 325°F for direct heat cooking.
7. Arrange the skewered steak unto the grill and grill 8 minutes or until the meat is done, turning occasionally.
8. Remove the skewered meat from the grill and let them sit for a few minutes to cool.
9. Serve warm and enjoy.

Nutrition Facts

Servings: 8

Amount per serving

Calories 321

	% Daily Value*
Total Fat 9.2g	12%
Saturated Fat 2.5g	12%
Cholesterol 102mg	34%
Sodium 954mg	41%

Nutrition Facts
Servings: 8

Total Carbohydrate 15.5g	**6%**
Dietary Fiber 0.3g	**1%**
Total Sugars 13.5g	
Protein 42.2g	
Vitamin D 0mcg	0%
Calcium 25mg	2%
Iron 4mg	24%
Potassium 454mg	10%

Smoked Italian Meatballs

PREP TIME: 10 minutes

COOK TIME: 30 minutes
SERVINGS: 6
Ingredients:
- 1 pound ground beef
- 1 pound Italian Sausage
- ½ cup Italian breadcrumbs
- 1 tsp dry mustard
- ½ cup parmesan cheese (grated)
- 1 tsp Italian seasoning
- 1 jalapeno (finely chopped)
- 2 eggs
- 1 tsp salt
- 1 onion (finely chopped)
- 2 tsp garlic powder
- ½ tsp smoked paprika
- 1 tsp oregano
- 1 tsp crushed red pepper
- 1 tbsp Worcestershire sauce

Directions:
1. Combine all the ingredients in a large mixing bowl. Mix until the ingredients are well combined.
2. Mold the mixture into 1 ½ inch balls and arrange the balls into a greased baking sheet.

3. Preheat the wood pellet smoker to 180°F, using hickory pellet.
4. Arrange the meatballs on the grill and smoke for 20 minutes.
5. Increase the griller's temperature to 350°F and smoke until the internal temperature of the meatballs reaches 165°F.
6. Remove the meatballs from the grill and let them cool for a few minutes.
7. Serve warm and enjoy.

Nutrition Facts

Servings: 6

Amount per serving

Calories 501

	% Daily Value*
Total Fat 30.4g	39%
Saturated Fat 10.5g	53%
Cholesterol 192mg	64%
Sodium 1196mg	52%
Total Carbohydrate 10.6g	4%
Dietary Fiber 1.3g	5%
Total Sugars 2.4g	
Protein 44g	

Nutrition Facts
Servings: 6

Vitamin D 5mcg	26%
Calcium 122mg	9%
Iron 16mg	90%
Potassium 625mg	13%

Prime Rib Roast

PREP TIME: 20 minutes
COOK TIME: 3 hours 30 minutes
SERVINGS: 12
Ingredients:
- 6 pounds boneless prime rib roast

- 2 tsp salt or more to taste
- 2 tsp ground black pepper or more to taste
- ½ cup olive oil
- 1/8 cup red wine vinegar
- 2 cups low sodium beef broth
- 1 tsp thyme
- 6 garlic cloves (minced)
- 2 tsp fresh rosemary

BBQ Rub:
- ½ cup brown sugar
- ½ tsp cayenne pepper
- 1 tbsp garlic powder
- 1 tbsp smoked paprika
- 2 tbsp paprika
- 1 tsp mustard powder
- 1 tbsp onion powder
- 1 tbsp black pepper
- 1 tbsp kosher salt

Directions:
1. Combine the garlic, thyme, rosemary, vinegar, oil, pepper and salt.
2. Pour the mixture into a zip-lock bag and add the prime roast. Refrigerate for about 6 hour or overnight.

3. Before roasting, remove the rib roast from the marinade and let it sit for about 2 hours or until it is at room temperature.
4. Meanwhile, combine all the ingredients for the rub in a mixing bowl.
5. Season the all sides of the rib with enough rub. Store the remaining rub in an airtight container for future use.
6. Place a v-shaped rack in a roasting pan and pour the beef broth into the bottom of the pan. Place the rib roast on the rack, fat side up.
7. Preheat your pellet grill on high heat with lid closed for 15 minutes. Use mesquite wood pellets.
8. Place the roasting pan on the grill. Roast for 30 minutes.
9. Reduce the heat to 250°F and roast for an additional 3 hours or until the rib roast's temperature reaches 130°F.
10. Remove the pan from the grill and let the roast sit for a few minutes to cool.
11. Transfer the roast to a cutting board and cut into sizes.

Nutrition Facts

Servings: 12

Amount per serving

Calories 737

	% Daily Value*
Total Fat 59.1g	76%
Saturated Fat 21.3g	106%
Cholesterol 161mg	54%
Sodium 638mg	28%
Total Carbohydrate 8.8g	3%
Dietary Fiber 0.8g	3%
Total Sugars 6.5g	
Protein 41.6g	
Vitamin D 0mcg	0%
Calcium 22mg	2%
Iron 6mg	34%
Potassium 101mg	2%

Beef Tenderloin

PREP TIME: 15 minutes
COOK TIME: 45 minutes
SERVINGS: 8
Ingredients:
- 4 pounds beef tenderloin
- 1 tbsp olive oil
- ½ tsp paprika
- 2 tsp Jacobsen salt
- ½ tsp ground cumin
- 1 tsp red pepper flakes
- 1 tsp ground black pepper
- 1 tsp fresh thyme
- ½ tsp oregano

  Mustard Cream Sauce:
- 1 tsp freshly ground black pepper
- 1 tsp oil

- 1 cup heavy cream
- ¼ cup shallot (chopped)
- 2 tsp chopped fresh basil
- 2 tsp chopped fresh dill
- 1 garlic clove (minced)
- 1 cup dry white wine
- 4 tbsp mustard
- 1 tsp Jacobsen salt

Directions:
1. In a small mixing bowl, combine the thyme, oregano, pepper flakes, black pepper, cumin, salt, paprika and oregano.
2. Rub all sides of the tenderloin with olive oil.
3. Sprinkle rub mixture over the tenderloin as needed. Make sure the tenderloin is coated in seasonings.
4. Preheat your pellet smoker grill on HIGH with lid closed. Use apple or maple wood pellet.
5. Place tenderloin on the grill grate and cook for about 15 minutes.
6. Reduce the grill temperature to 375°F and cook for an additional 30 minutes or until the tenderloin's temperature reaches 130°F.
7. Remove the tenderloin from heat and let it rest for a few minutes to cool.

8. For the mustard sauce, heat up the olive oil in a saucepan over medium to high heat.
9. Add the shallot and garlic. Saute until the veggies are tender.
10. Stir in the mustard, black pepper and wine.
11. Bring to a boil, reduce the heat and simmer until the sauce thickens, stirring often.
12. Remove the saucepan from heat and stir in the heavy cream, basil, dill, salt and pepper.
13. Cut the tenderloin into sizes and serve with mustard sauce.

Nutrition Facts

Servings: 8

Amount per serving

Calories 598

	% Daily Value*
Total Fat 30.4g	39%
Saturated Fat 11.7g	59%
Cholesterol 229mg	76%
Sodium 1015mg	44%
Total Carbohydrate 5g	2%
Dietary Fiber 1.2g	4%
Total Sugars 0.7g	
Protein 67.8g	

Nutrition Facts
Servings: 8

Vitamin D 8mcg	39%
Calcium 93mg	7%
Iron 6mg	32%
Potassium 935mg	20%

Beef Stuffed Bell Pepper

PREP TIME: 15 minutes
COOK TIME: 45 minutes
SERVINGS: 4
Ingredients:
- 4 large red bell pepper
- ½ cups cooked rice

- 1 small onion (diced)
- 1 tsp chili powder
- 1 tomato (finely chopped)
- 1 tsp olive oil
- ¼ tsp ground black pepper or to taste
- ¼ tsp red pepper flakes
- ½ tsp salt
- ¼ tsp garlic
- 1-pound ground beef
- 1 cup shredded parmesan cheese
- 4 tbsp ketchup
- ½ cup dry quick oats

Directions:
1. Cut of the top of the pepper and scoop out the pepper membrane and seeds.
2. Heat up the olive oil in a large skillet over medium to high heat. Add the onion and sliced tomatoes. Saute until the onion is tender.
3. Add the ground beef and cook until the ground beef is pink, breaking the beef apart while cooking.
4. Remove the skillet from heat and stir in the salt, garlic, ketchup, pepper, rice, oat, pepper flakes, and chili powder.

5. Start the grill on a smoker mode and leave opened for 5 minutes or until fire has started.
6. Close the lid and preheat it to 350°F, using mesquite wood pellet.
7. Arrange the stuffed pepper on the grill grate, stuffed side up. Cook stuffed peppers for about 40 minutes.
8. Top each stuffed pepper with parmesan cheese and cook for an additional 5 minutes or until the cheese is melted.

Nutrition Facts

Servings: 4

Amount per serving

Calories 490

	% Daily Value*
Total Fat 15g	19%
Saturated Fat 6.6g	33%
Cholesterol 119mg	40%
Sodium 778mg	34%
Total Carbohydrate 41.9g	15%
Dietary Fiber 3.8g	14%
Total Sugars 10.8g	
Protein 47.3g	

Nutrition Facts
Servings: 4

Vitamin D 0mcg	0%
Calcium 258mg	20%
Iron 24mg	131%
Potassium 881mg	19%

Braised Beef Short ribs

PREP TIME: 15 minutes
COOK TIME: 3 hours 20 minutes
SERVINGS: 8
Ingredients:
- 2 tbsp olive oil
- 1 carrot (chopped)

- 2 red bell pepper (sliced)
- 1 onion (chopped)
- 2 tbsp balsamic vinegar
- 4 pounds beef short ribs
- ½ tsp pepper
- 2 cups red wine
- 3 cups beef broth
- 1 tsp thyme
- ½ tsp paprika
- ½ tsp garlic powder
- 1 tsp salt or to taste
- ½ tsp onion powder
- 2 tsp dried peppermint

Directions:
1. Configure your wood pellet grill to smoke mode and leave the grill lid opened until fire starts.
2. Close the lid and preheat grill to HIGH with lid closed for 15 minutes, use apple or maple wood pellet.
3. Season all sides of the short rib generously with salt, onion powder, garlic powder and pepper. Place the rib on the grill grate and smoke for 10 minutes or until the rib is browned. Turn ribs after the first 5 minutes.

4. Remove the ribs from the grill and reduce the heat to 350°F.
5. Heat up the olive oil in a large Dutch grill over medium to high heat.
6. Add the onion, celery and garlic. Saute for about 4 minutes or until the veggies are tender and fragrant. Stir constantly.
7. Add the tomato, carrot, bay leaves, and red bell pepper. Cook for 6 minutes, stirring often.
8. Pour in the red wine and balsamic vinegar. Stir to combine. Cook until the sauce thickens.
9. Pour in the beef broth and stir in the paprika, peppermint and thyme.
10. Cover the Dutch grill tightly with aluminum foil and place it on the grill.
11. Braise at 350°F for 3 hours or until the meat is fork tender.
12. Remove the Dutch grill from heat and let the ribs sit for a few minutes to cool.
13. Use a slotted spoon to transfer the beef to a bowl. Close the bowl and set aside.
14. Stain the broth through a fine mesh strainer. Press the vegetables to the mesh with a flat spoon to extract all juice.

15. Transfer the juice to a Dutch grill. Bring to a boil over medium to high heat. Reduce heat and simmer until the sauce thicken and has reduced by half.
16. Add the short ribs to the sauce and cook for 1 minute.
17. Remove the Dutch grill from heat.
18. Serve and enjoy.

Nutrition Facts

Servings: 8

Amount per serving

Calories 580

	% Daily Value*
Total Fat 24.6g	31%
Saturated Fat 8.4g	42%
Cholesterol 206mg	69%
Sodium 723mg	31%
Total Carbohydrate 6.8g	2%
Dietary Fiber 1.1g	4%
Total Sugars 3.3g	
Protein 68g	

Grilled Filet Mignon

PREP TIME: 5 minutes
COOK TIME: 15 minutes
SERVINGS: 3
Ingredients:
- 3 filet mignons
- 3 tbsp butter (melted)
- 2 cloves garlic (minced)
- 2 tsp dried rosemary
- 1 tsp salt or more to taste
- 2 tsp ground black pepper to taste

Directions:
1. Combine the butter, rosemary, pepper, salt and garlic in a small mixing bowl. Mix thoroughly.

2. Rub all sides of the filet mignon with the mixture.
3. Preheat your wood pellet grill to 450°F with lid closed for 15 minutes, using hickory wood pellets.
4. Arrange the filet mignons directly on the grill grate.
5. Cook both mignons for 5-8 minutes per side, or until the meat temperature reaches 140°F.
6. Remove the filet mignons from heat and let them rest for a few minutes to cool.
7. Enjoy.

Nutrition Facts
Servings: 3

Amount per serving

Calories	**263**
	% Daily Value*
Total Fat 17.3g	22%
Saturated Fat 9.5g	47%
Cholesterol 87mg	29%
Sodium 908mg	39%
Total Carbohydrate 2.1g	1%
Dietary Fiber 0.8g	3%

Nutrition Facts
Servings: 3

   Total Sugars 0g

Protein 24.3g

Vitamin D 8mcg	40%
Calcium 41mg	3%
Iron 2mg	12%
Potassium 351mg	7%

Hickory Rack of Lamb

PREP TIME: 10 minutes
COOK TIME: 2 hours

SERVINGS: 3

Ingredients:
- 1 (3 pounds) rack of lamb (frenched)

Marinade Ingredients:
- 1 lemon (juiced)
- 1 tsp ground black pepper
- 1 tsp thyme
- ¼ cup balsamic vinegar
- 1 tsp dried basil
- 2 tbsp Dijon mustard
- 2 cloves garlic (crushed)

Rub Ingredients:
- ½ tsp cayenne pepper
- ½ tsp ground black pepper
- ¼ tsp Italian seasoning
- 1 tsp oregano
- 1 tsp dried mint
- 1 tsp paprika
- 1 tsp garlic powder
- 1 tsp onion powder
- 1 tsp dried parsley
- 1 tsp dried basil
- 1 tsp dried rosemary
- 4 tbsp olive oil

Directions:

1. Combine all the marinade ingredients in a mixing bowl. Pour the marinade into a gallon zip-lock bag. Add the rack of lamb and massage the marinade into the rack. Seal the bag and place it in a refrigerator. Refrigerate for 8 hour or overnight.
2. When ready to roast, remove the rack of lamb from the marinade and let it sit for about 2 hour or until it is at room temperature.
3. Meanwhile, combine all the rub ingredients except the olive oil in a mixing bowl.
4. Rub the rub mixture over the rack of lamb generously. Drizzle rack with the olive oil.
5. Start your grill on smoke with the lid opened until fire starts.
6. Close the lid and preheat grill to 225°F using hickory wood pellets.
7. Place the rack of lamb on the grill grate, bone side down. Smoke for about 2 hours or until the internal temperature of the meat reaches 140-145°F.
8. Remove the rack of lamb from the grill and let it rest for about 10 minutes to cool.

Nutrition Facts
Servings: 3

Amount per serving
Calories 800

	% Daily Value*
Total Fat 41.1g	53%
Saturated Fat 14.2g	71%
Cholesterol 301mg	100%
Sodium 444mg	19%
Total Carbohydrate 6.7g	2%
Dietary Fiber 2.2g	8%
Total Sugars 1.4g	
Protein 93.8g	
Vitamin D 0mcg	0%
Calcium 128mg	10%
Iron 9mg	50%
Potassium 139mg	3%

Leg of Lamb

PREP TIME: 10 minutes
COOK TIME: 2 hours
SERVINGS: 6
Ingredients:
- 1 (2 pounds) leg of lamb
- 1 tsp dried rosemary
- 2 tsp freshly ground black pepper
- 4 cloves garlic (minced)

- 2 tsp salt or more to taste
- ½ tsp paprika
- 1 tsp thyme
- 2 tbsp olive oil
- 1 tsp brown sugar
- 2 tbsp oregano

Directions:
1. Trim the meat of excess fat and remove silver-skin.
2. In a mixing bowl, combine the thyme, salt, sugar, oregano, paprika, black pepper, garlic and olive oil.
3. Generously, rub the mixture over the leg of lamb. Cover seasoned leg of lamb with foil and let it sit for 1 hour to marinate.
4. Start your grill on smoke and leave the lid open for 5 minutes, or until fire starts. Cover the lid and preheat grill to 250°F using hickory, maple or apple wood pellets.
5. Remove the foil and place the leg of lamb on a smoker rack. Place the rack on the grill and smoke the leg of lamb for about 4 hours, or until the internal temperature of the meat reaches 145°F.
6. Remove the leg of lamb from the grill and let it rest for a few minutes to cool.

7. Cut into sizes and serve.

Nutrition Facts

Servings: 6

Amount per serving
Calories 334

% Daily Value*

Total Fat 16g 21%

　Saturated Fat 4.7g 23%

Cholesterol 136mg 45%

Sodium 891mg 39%

Total Carbohydrate 2.9g 1%

　Dietary Fiber 1.1g 4%

　Total Sugars 0.6g

Protein 42.9g

Vitamin D 0mcg 0%

Calcium 57mg 4%

Iron 5mg 26%

Potassium 557mg 12%

BBQ Burnt Ends

PREP TIME: 15 minutes
COOK TIME: 8 hours
SERVINGS: 12
Ingredients:
- 2 tbsp olive oil
- 5 pounds brisket point

- 4 tbsp brown sugar
- ¼ tsp cayenne pepper
- ½ tsp onion powder
- ½ tsp garlic powder
- 1 tbsp paprika
- 1 tsp oregano
- 1 tbsp freshly ground black pepper
- 2 tbsp salt or to taste
- 1 tsp dried peppermint
- 2 cups beef broth
- 2 tbsp butter (softened)
- 1 cup BBQ sauce
- 5 ½ tbsp honey

Directions:
1. Trim the brisket point of any excess fat.
2. To make the rub, combine the sugar, cayenne, onion powder, garlic, paprika, oregano, peppermint, pepper and salt in a mixing bowl.
3. Drizzle the brisket with the olive oil. Sprinkle all sides of the brisket point generously with the rub mixture.
4. Preheat your wood pellet grill to 250°F with lid closed for 15 minutes. Use hickory or oak wood pellets.

5. Place the brisket point on the grill grate and cook for about 6 hours, or until the internal temperature of the meat reaches 190°F.
6. Remove brisket from heat and cut it into 1-inch cubes.
7. Combine the butter, honey and BBQ sauce in a pan. Add the brisket cubes and toss to combine. Cover the pan with aluminum foil and place it on the grill. Cook for 1 hour.
8. Remove the aluminum foil cover and stir the beef cubes. Cook, uncovered, for 1 hour.
9. Remove the pan from heat and let the burnt ends cool for a few minutes.
10. Serve and enjoy.

Nutrition Facts

Servings: 12

Amount per serving	
Calories	**613**
	% Daily Value*
Total Fat 34.3g	44%
Saturated Fat 12.8g	64%
Cholesterol 177mg	59%
Sodium 1684mg	73%
Total Carbohydrate 19.5g	7%

Nutrition Facts
Servings: 12

Dietary Fiber 0.6g	**2%**
Total Sugars 16.5g	
Protein 54.1g	
Vitamin D 1mcg	7%
Calcium 26mg	2%
Iron 6mg	32%
Potassium 630mg	13%

Smoked Pulled Beef

PREP TIME: 15 minutes
COOK TIME: 9 hours
SERVINGS: 6
Ingredients:
- 4 pounds beef sirloin tip roast (trimmed of excess fat)
- 2 tbsp kosher salt
- 2 tbsp garlic powder
- 1 tbsp ground black pepper
- 1 tbsp cayenne pepper
- 1 tsp paprika

- 1 tsp oregano
- 1 onion (chopped)
- 2 cups beef broth

Directions:
1. To make rub, combine the cayenne, black pepper, garlic, paprika and salt in a small mixing bowl.
2. Rub the meat with the rub mixture generously. The sirloin should be coated with rub.
3. Preheat the grill to 225°F with lid closed for 15 minutes. Use a fruit wood pellet.
4. Place the sirloin directly on the grill, fat side up, and smoke 4 hours. Flip roast frequently after the first one of smoking.
5. Remove the sirloin from heat adjust the grill temperature to 250°F.
6. Combine the chopped onion and beef broth in a large disposable aluminum foil. Add the roast.
7. Place the pan on the grill and cook for about 3 hour or until the internal temperature of the meat reaches 165°F.
8. Tear off a large portion of aluminum foil and use it to cover the pan tightly. Cook for

an additional 3 hour or until the internal temperature of the meat reaches 200°F.
9. Remove the pan from the heat and leave the meat to cool for few minutes.
10. Drain the braising liquid from the pan, reserving 1 ½ cups of the liquid.
11. Run the reserved braising liquid through a fat separator to remove excess fat.
12. Shred the roast using two forks. Pour in the reserved braising liquid into the pan.
13. Serve and enjoy.

Nutrition Facts
Servings: 6

Amount per serving
Calories 599

	% Daily Value*
Total Fat 19.6g	25%
Saturated Fat 7.3g	37%
Cholesterol 270mg	90%
Sodium 1619mg	70%
Total Carbohydrate 5.6g	2%
Dietary Fiber 1.4g	5%
Total Sugars 1.8g	
Protein 94.3g	

Nutrition Facts
Servings: 6

Vitamin D 0mcg	0%
Calcium 24mg	2%
Iron 58mg	321%
Potassium 1388mg	30%

Beef Chili

PREP TIME: 20 minutes
COOK TIME: 1 hour 30 minutes

SERVINGS: 8
Ingredients:
- 2 pound ground beef
- 2 tbsp olive oil
- 1 tbsp chili powder
- 1 can stewed tomatoes
- 1 can (28 ounces) diced tomatoes
- 2 tbsp tomato paste
- 2 cans ranch style beans
- 1 medium onion (chopped)
- 1 red bell pepper (chopped)
- 1 green bell pepper (chopped)
- 2 medium jalapeno pepper (thinly sliced)
- 3 garlic cloves (minced)
- 2 tsp cumin
- 1 tsp oregano
- ½ tsp ground black pepper or to taste
- ½ tsp Italian seasoning
- 1 tsp pink salt
- 1 tsp Worcestershire sauce
- Sour cream for serving

Directions:
1. Preheat your grill to 250°F with lid closed for 15 minutes, using apple or maple hardwood pellet.

2. Heat up a large Dutch grill over medium to high heat. Add the ground beef and saute until it is browned, breaking it apart with a spoon while sautéing. Use a slotted spoon to transfer the beef to a paper towel lined plate to drain. Discard excess fat from the Dutch grill.
3. Add oil to the Dutch grill. Once the oil is hot, add the onions, green pepper, red pepper, jalapeno, and garlic. Saute until the veggies are tender.
4. Add the tomato paste and cook for 1 minute, stirring often.
5. Stir in the diced tomatoes, beans, Worcestershire sauce, salt, Italian seasoning, oregano, pepper, cumin and chili powder.
6. Bring mixture to a boil, reduce the heat and simmer for about 10 minutes.
7. Remove the Dutch grill from stovetop, cover it and place it on the grill grate.
8. Cook for about 1 hour.
9. Remove the Dutch grill from heat and let the chili sit for a few minutes.
10. Serve warm and top with sour cream

Nutrition Facts
Servings: 8

Amount per serving
Calories 290

	% Daily Value*
Total Fat 11.5g	**15%**
Saturated Fat 3.4g	**17%**
Cholesterol 102mg	**34%**
Sodium 481mg	**21%**
Total Carbohydrate 9.5g	**3%**
Dietary Fiber 2.6g	**9%**
Total Sugars 3.7g	
Protein 36.3g	
Vitamin D 0mcg	0%
Calcium 33mg	3%
Iron 23mg	125%
Potassium 651mg	14%

Stuffed Flank Steak

PREP TIME: 20 minutes
COOK TIME: 20 minutes
SERVINGS: 4
Ingredients:
- 1 (3 pounds) flank steak (trimmed of excess fat)
- 5 ounces goat cheese
- 1 tsp granulated garlic
- 1 red bell pepper (finely chopped)
- 6 slices of prosciutto

- 1 cup fresh parsley (finely chopped)
- 1 tsp salt or to taste
- 1 tsp ground black pepper
- 2 tbsp olive oil

Rub:
- ½ cup brown sugar
- ½ tsp cayenne pepper
- ½ tsp garlic powder
- ½ tbsp smoked paprika
- 1 tsp mustard powder
- ¼ tsp onion powder
- ¼ tsp black pepper
- ½ tsp kosher salt

Directions:
1. Carefully butterfly the flank steak. Place the flank steak on a flat surface, cut side up. Place a plastic wrap over it and pound the meat with a mallet until it is evenly flattened. Remove the plastic wrap.
2. Season the flank steak generously with salt and pepper.
3. Layer the prosciutto slices on the flank steak.
4. Spread the granulated garlic, red bell pepper and chopped parsley over the flank steak.
5. Top the with goat cheese.

6. Roll up the flank steak. Tie the rolled flank steak with butcher's twine at 2-inch interval. Brush all sides of the rolled meat with olive oil.
7. Preheat your grill to HIGH (450°F) with lid closed for 15 minutes.
8. Place the stuffed flank steak on the grill and cook for 20 minutes, 10 minutes per side.
9. Remove the steak from heat let it rest for about 12 minutes.
10. Remove the butcher's brine and cut the steak to slices.
11. Serve.

Nutrition Facts
Servings: 4

Amount per serving
Calories 737

	% Daily Value*
Total Fat 42.9g	55%
Saturated Fat 18.9g	95%
Cholesterol 193mg	64%
Sodium 2434mg	106%
Total Carbohydrate 23.4g	8%
Dietary Fiber 1.6g	6%
Total Sugars 20.3g	

Nutrition Facts
Servings: 4

Protein 65.7g

Vitamin D 0mcg	0%
Calcium 365mg	28%
Iron 6mg	34%
Potassium 658mg	14%

Beef Bourguignon

PREP TIME: 45 minutes
COOK TIME: 4 hours

SERVINGS: 12
Ingredients:
- 1 tsp smoked paprika
- 2 tbsp butter
- 1 tsp salt
- 1 tbsp fresh rosemary
- 1 tbsp fresh thyme
- 1 tbsp fresh cracked pepper
- 6 cups low sodium beef broth
- 4 pound beef chuck roast (cubed)
- 1 pound bacon (cut into 2 inch chunks)
- 2 cups dry red wine
- 6 cloves garlic (chopped)
- 2 pints mushrooms (slightly chopped)
- 2 tbsp Worcestershire sauce
- 2 tbsp tomato paste
- 2 cups chopped onions
- 2 cups sliced carrot

Directions:
1. When ready to cook, preheat your grill to 350°F with lid closed for 15 minutes.
2. Heat up a nonstick Dutch grill over medium to high heat.
3. Add the bacon and saute until the bacon is crispy, stirring often.

4. Use a slotted spoon to transfer the bacon to a paper towel lined plate to drain.
5. Add the carrot, onion, garlic, rosemary, thyme, cracked pepper and paprika. Saute until the veggies are tender and the onion pieces turn golden brown.
6. Add the tomato paste and cook for 1 more minute.
7. Use a spoon to transfer the cooked vegetables to a separate bowl. Set aside.
8. Add the cubed beef chuck to the pot and sear until browned.
9. Pour in the beef broth and stir in the Worcestershire sauce and red wine.
10. Stir with a wooden spoon, scraping the bottom and sides of the pot while stirring.
11. Stir in the roasted vegetable and crispy bacon.
12. Bring to a boil and simmer for a few minutes.
13. Cover the Dutch grill and place it on the preheated grill. Close the grill.
14. Cook for about 2 to 3 hours until the beef is tender, stirring the bourguignon every 30 minutes.

15. Meanwhile, melt the butter in a frying pan over medium to high heat.
16. Add the mushrooms and saute until the mushrooms are just tender. Set aside.
17. Once the beef is tender, remove the pot from the grill and stir in the mushrooms.
18. Return the Dutch grill to the grill and cook for about 20 minutes, uncovered.
19. Remove the Dutch grill from the heat and leave the bourguignon to cool for about 10 minutes.
20. Serve.

Nutrition Facts

Servings: 12

Amount per serving
Calories 857

	% Daily Value*
Total Fat 60.8g	78%
Saturated Fat 23.4g	117%
Cholesterol 202mg	67%
Sodium 1616mg	70%
Total Carbohydrate 9.2g	3%
Dietary Fiber 1.5g	6%

Nutrition Facts

Servings: 12

Total Sugars 3.7g

Protein 57.5g

Vitamin D 85mcg	427%
Calcium 57mg	4%
Iron 7mg	38%
Potassium 905mg	19%

Beef Stew

PREP TIME: 20 minutes
COOK TIME: 4 hours
SERVINGS: 6
Ingredients:
- 1 ½ pound trimmed beef chuck roast (cut into 1-inch cubes)
- 4 stalks celery (chopped)
- 1 pound radish (halved)

- 1 large onion sliced
- 3 tbsp olive oil
- 3 ounces carrot (sliced)
- 2 tbsp tomato paste
- 6 cups beef broth
- 1 tsp salt or to taste
- 1 bay leaf
- 1 tsp pepper or to taste
- 2 cloves garlic (chopped)
- ½ tsp thyme

Directions:
1. Heat up the olive oil in a large Dutch grill over medium to high heat.
2. Add the onions, carrot, garlic and celery. Saute until the onion is translucent.
3. Use a slotted spoon to transfer the vegetables to a separate bowl.
4. Add the cubed beef and saute until the beef cubes are browned.
5. Add the thyme, pepper, salt, tomato paste and bay leaf.
6. Cook for about 30 seconds, stirring until the beef cubes are coated.

7. Deglaze the Dutch grill with 1 cup beef broth, scrapping the button and sides of the Dutch grill with a wooden spoon.
8. Pour in the remaining beef broth and stir. Cover the Dutch grill.
9. Start your grill on smoke mode, leaving the lid opened for 5 minutes, until fire starts.
10. Close the lid and preheat grill to 300°F, using pecan hardwood pellets.
11. Place the Dutch grill on the grill and cook for 2 hours.
12. Add the roasted vegetables and radish. Cook for another 2 hours or until beef is tender.
13. Remove the Dutch grill from heat and let it sit for a few minutes.
14. Discard the bay leaf and serve.

Nutrition Facts

Servings: 6

Amount per serving

Calories   **512**

% Daily Value*

Total Fat 35.6g	46%
Saturated Fat 12.1g	60%

Nutrition Facts
Servings: 6

Cholesterol 112mg	**37%**
Sodium 1274mg	**55%**
Total Carbohydrate 9.2g	**3%**
Dietary Fiber 2.7g	**10%**
Total Sugars 4.7g	
Protein 37.3g	
Vitamin D 0mcg	0%
Calcium 63mg	5%
Iron 5mg	27%
Potassium 837mg	18%

Chapter Two

Poultry Recipes

Beef Can Smoked Chicken

PREP TIME: 15 minutes
COOK TIME: 75 minutes
SERVINGS: 5
Ingredients:

- 1 (4 pounds) chicken
- 1 can beer
- 1 tsp onion powder
- 1 tsp Greek seasoning
- ½ tsp oregano
- 1 tsp smoked paprika
- 1 tsp garlic powder
- 1 tsp salt or more to taste
- 2 tbsp olive oil

Directions:
1. Remove the neck and giblets from the chicken. Discard it.
2. Rinse the chicken thoroughly with water and pat it dry with paper towels.
3. Rub the olive oil all over the chicken. Rub it into the cavity as well.
4. Combine the onion powder, salt, garlic, paprika, Greek seasoning and oregano.
5. Rub the seasoning mix all over the chicken. Rub into the cavity as well.
6. Open the beer can and discard half of the beer.
7. Insert the beer can into the chicken cavity, in between the chicken legs. Use the chicken leg as a tripod to hold the chicken up.

8. Start your grill on smoke, leaving the lid opened until fire starts.
9. Close the lid and preheat the grill to 350°F, using mesquite hardwood pellets.
10. Set the chicken on a sheet tray, beer side down. Place the sheet on the grill and for about 75 minutes or until the internal temperature of the chicken reaches 165°F.
11. Remove the chicken from heat and let it rest for a few minutes.
12. Serve beer chicken and enjoy.

Nutrition Facts

Servings: 5

Amount per serving

Calories 633

	% Daily Value*
Total Fat 16.7g	21%
Saturated Fat 3.9g	19%
Cholesterol 279mg	93%
Sodium 729mg	32%
Total Carbohydrate 4g	1%
Dietary Fiber 0.3g	1%
Total Sugars 0.4g	
Protein 105.8g	

Nutrition Facts
Servings: 5

Vitamin D 0mcg	0%
Calcium 56mg	4%
Iron 3mg	19%
Potassium 725mg	15%

Marinated Smoked Turkey Breast

PREP TIME: 15 minutes
COOK TIME: 4 hours
SERVINGS: 6
Ingredients:

- 1 (5 pounds) boneless chicken breast
- 4 cups water
- 2 tbsp kosher salt
- 1 tsp Italian seasoning
- 2 tbsp honey
- 1 tbsp cider vinegar

Rub:
- ½ tsp onion powder
- 1 tsp paprika
- 1 tsp salt
- 1 tsp ground black pepper
- 1 tbsp brown sugar
- ½ tsp garlic powder
- 1 tsp oregano

Directions:
1. In a large mixing bowl, combine the water, honey, cider vinegar, Italian seasoning and salt.
2. Add the chicken breast and toss to combine. Cover the bowl and place it in the refrigerator and chill for 4 hours.
3. Rinse the chicken breast with water and pat dry with paper towels.
4. In another mixing bowl, combine the brown sugar, salt, paprika, onion powder, pepper, oregano and garlic.

5. Generously season the chicken breasts with the rub mix.
6. Preheat the grill to 225°F with lid closed for 15 minutes. Use cherry wood pellets.
7. Arrange the turkey breast into a grill rack. Place the grill rack on the grill.
8. Smoke for about 3 to 4 hours or until the internal temperature of the turkey breast reaches 165°F.
9. Remove the chicken breast from heat and let them rest for a few minutes.
10. Serve.

Nutrition Facts
Servings: 5

Amount per serving
Calories 903

	% Daily Value*
Total Fat 34g	44%
Saturated Fat 9.3g	47%
Cholesterol 404mg	135%
Sodium 1328mg	58%
Total Carbohydrate 9.9g	4%
Dietary Fiber 0.5g	2%
Total Sugars 9g	

Nutrition Facts
Servings: 5

Protein 131.5g

Vitamin D 0mcg	0%
Calcium 85mg	7%
Iron 6mg	33%

Maple Bourbon Turkey

PREP TIME: 15 minutes
COOK TIME: 3 hours
SERVINGS: 8
Ingredients:

- 1 (12 pounds) turkey
- 8 cup chicken broth
- 1 stick butter (softened)
- 1 tsp thyme
- 2 garlic clove (minced)
- 1 tsp dried basil
- 1 tsp pepper
- 1 tsp salt
- 1 tbsp minced rosemary
- 1 tsp paprika
- 1 lemon (wedged)
- 1 onion
- 1 orange (wedged)
- 1 apple (wedged)

Maple Bourbon Glaze:
- ¾ cup bourbon
- 1/2 cup maple syrup
- 1 stick butter (melted)
- 1 tbsp lime

Directions:
1. Rinse the turkey inside and out under cold running water.
2. Insert the onion, lemon, orange and apple into the turkey cavity.

3. In a mixing bowl, combine the butter, paprika, thyme, garlic, basil, pepper, salt, basil and rosemary.
4. Brush the turkey generously with the herb-butter mixture.
5. Set a rack into a roasting pan and place the turkey on the rack. Pour 5 cups of chicken broth into the bottom of the roasting pan.
6. Preheat the grill to 350°F with lid closed for 15 minutes, using maple wood pellets.
7. Place the roasting pan in the grill and cook for 1 hour.
8. Meanwhile, combine all the maple bourbon glaze ingredients in a mixing bowl. Mix until well combined.
9. Baste the turkey with glaze mixture. Continue cooking, basting turkey every 30 minutes and adding more broth as needed for 2 hours, or until the internal temperature of the turkey reaches 165°F.
10. Remove the turkey from the grill and let it rest for a few minutes.
11. Cut into slices and serve.

Nutrition Facts
Servings: 8

Amount per serving

Nutrition Facts
Servings: 8
Calories   1536

	% Daily Value*
Total Fat 58.6g	**75%**
Saturated Fat 26.1g	**131%**
Cholesterol 576mg	**192%**
Sodium 1697mg	**74%**
Total Carbohydrate 24g	**9%**
Dietary Fiber 2.3g	**8%**
Total Sugars 18.4g	
Protein 205.1g	
Vitamin D 16mcg	79%
Calcium 76mg	6%
Iron 69mg	386%
Potassium 2405mg	51%

Huli Huli Chicken

PREP TIME: 20 minutes
COOK TIME: 2 hours 30 minutes
SERVINGS: 10
Ingredients:
- 4 pounds boneless skinless chicken thighs
- 1/3 cup ketchup
- 1 cup pineapple juice
- ½ cup soy sauce
- ½ cup brown sugar
- 2 tbsp minced ginger
- 2 tbsp Worcestershire sauce
- 2 garlic cloves (minced)

Garnish:
- 4 tbsp chopped green onions

Directions:
1. In a mixing bowl, combine the soy sauce, brown sugar, ketchup, soy sauce, ginger, ketchup, Worcestershire sauce, pineapple juice and garlic.
2. Pour 1 cup of the mixture into a gallon size zip-lock bag. Add the chicken thighs and massage the marinade into the thighs. Seal the bag and refrigerate for 1 hour.
3. Meanwhile, pour the remaining marinade mixture into a saucepan over medium to high heat. Bring to a boil, reduce the heat and simmer until the sauce thickens.
4. Remove the saucepan from heat.
5. Remove the thighs from the marinade and let them rest for about an hour or until they are at room temperature.
6. Preheat your grill to 250°F with lid closed for 10-15 minutes. Use apple hardwood pellets.
7. Arrange thighs on the grill grate and cook for 2 hours. Flip half way through.
8. Brush reserved sauce over chicken thighs generously. Cook for 30 minutes more or

until the internal temperature of the thighs reaches 165°F.
9. Remove the wings from the heat and let them rest for a few minutes.
10. Serve and garnish with chopped green onions.

Nutrition Facts

Servings: 10

Amount per serving

Calories   408

% Daily Value*

Total Fat 13.6g	17%
Saturated Fat 3.7g	19%
Cholesterol 161mg	54%
Sodium 1000mg	43%
Total Carbohydrate 14.9g	5%
Dietary Fiber 0.3g	1%
Total Sugars 12.2g	
Protein 53.7g	
Vitamin D 0mcg	0%
Calcium 43mg	3%
Iron 3mg	15%
Potassium 558mg	12%

Herb Smoked Chicken

PREP TIME: 10 minutes
COOK TIME: 16 minutes
SERVINGS: 6
Ingredients:
- 3 tbsp olive oil
- 1 tsp thyme
- 1 tsp ground black pepper or to taste
- 4 tbsp freshly squeezed lemon juice
- 1 tbsp lemon zest
- 1 tbsp freshly chopped parsley

- 1 tsp salt or taste
- 1 tbsp chopped rosemary
- 2 tbsp freshly chopped cilantro
- 6 boneless chicken breasts

Directions:
1. In a large mixing bowl, combine the thyme, oil, pepper, juice, lemon zest, parsley, rosemary, cilantro and salt. Add the chicken breast and toss to combine. Cover the mixing bowl and refrigerate for 1 hour.
2. Remove the chicken breast from the marinade and let it rest for a few minutes, until it is at room temperature.
3. Start your grill on smoke, leaving the lid opened for 5 minutes or until fire starts.
4. Close the lid and preheat grill to 450°F with lid closed for 10-15 minutes, using mesquite wood pellets.
5. Arrange the chicken breasts onto the grill grate and smoke for 16 minutes, 8 minutes per side, or until the internal temperature of the chicken reaches 165°F.
6. Remove the chicken breasts from the grill and let them rest for a few minutes.
7. Serve and top with your favorite sauce.

Nutrition Facts

Servings: 6

Amount per serving
Calories 207

% Daily Value*

Total Fat 11.2g	14%
Saturated Fat 2.6g	13%
Cholesterol 65mg	22%
Sodium 431mg	19%
Total Carbohydrate 1.2g	0%
Dietary Fiber 0.5g	2%
Total Sugars 0.3g	
Protein 25.2g	
Vitamin D 0mcg	0%
Calcium 14mg	1%
Iron 1mg	7%
Potassium 32mg	1%

Honey Sesame Chicken Wings

PREP TIME: 10 minutes
COOK TIME: 15 minutes
SERVINGS: 4
Ingredients:
- 2 pounds chicken wings (trimmed)
- ½ tsp red pepper flakes
- ½ tsp ground black pepper
- ¼ cups honey
- 2 tsp rice wine vinegar
- 1 tbsp olive oil
- 1 tsp sesame oil

- 2 garlic cloves (minced)
- 1 tbsp chopped fresh ginger
- 3 scallions (chopped)
- 1 tbsp toasted sesame seeds

Directions:
1. In a large mixing bowl, combine the pepper flakes, black pepper, honey, wine vinegar, oil, sesame oil, garlic and ginger.
2. Pour mixture into a zip-lock bag, reserving ¼ cup of the marinade. Add the chicken wings and massage the marinade into the wings. Lock the bag and refrigerate for 3 to 4 hours.
3. Remove the wings from the marinade and let them rest for about one hour, until they are at room temperature. Pat the wings dry with paper towels.
4. Preheat the grill to 350°F with lid closed for 10-15 minutes.
5. Arrange the wings onto the grill. Cook for 15 minutes. Flip halfway through and baste with reserved marinate.
6. Remove the grill and let the rest for a few minutes.
7. Serve and garnish with sesame seed and scallions.

Nutrition Facts

Servings: 4

Amount per serving

Calories 562

	% Daily Value*
Total Fat 22.7g	29%
Saturated Fat 5.5g	27%
Cholesterol 202mg	67%
Sodium 199mg	9%
Total Carbohydrate 20.6g	7%
Dietary Fiber 0.9g	3%
Total Sugars 17.8g	
Protein 66.6g	
Vitamin D 0mcg	0%
Calcium 71mg	5%
Iron 4mg	20%
Potassium 636mg	14%

Cornish Game Hen

PREP TIME: 10 minutes
COOK TIME: 1 hour
SERVINGS: 6
Ingredients:
- 4 Cornish game hens
- 1 tsp paprika
- 1 tsp kosher salt
- 1 tsp thyme
- 1 tsp cayenne pepper
- 1 tsp garlic powder
- 1 tsp ground pepper
- 4 tbsp butter (melted)
- 2 tbsp freshly chopped parsley

Directions:
1. Rinse the game hens, inside and out, under cold running water.
2. Tuck the hen wings to the back and tie the legs together with butcher's string.
3. To make rub, combine the thyme, salt, paprika, cayenne, garlic powder, and ground pepper in a small mixing bowl.
4. Brush butter over the outer part of each game hen. Season hens generously with rub mix.
5. Start your grill on smoke, leaving the lid opened for 5 minutes or until fire starts.
6. Close the lid and preheat the grill to 375°F for 15 minutes, using mesquite hardwood pellets.
7. Place the hens on the grill and roast for 1 hour or until the internal temperature of the game hens reaches 165°F.
8. Remove the game hens from the grill and let them rest for a few minutes.
9. Cut into sizes and serve. Garnish with chopped fresh parsley.

Nutrition Facts
Servings: 6

Amount per serving

Nutrition Facts
Servings: 6

Calories 220

	% Daily Value*
Total Fat 18.5g	24%
Saturated Fat 4.9g	24%
Cholesterol 97mg	32%
Sodium 490mg	21%
Total Carbohydrate 1.1g	0%
Dietary Fiber 0.5g	2%
Total Sugars 0.2g	
Protein 13g	
Vitamin D 5mcg	27%
Calcium 10mg	1%
Iron 1mg	5%
Potassium 35mg	1%

BBQ Pulled Chicken

PREP TIME: 15 minutes
COOK TIME: 2 hours
SERVINGS: 4
Ingredients:

- 3 pounds whole chicken (halved and backbone removed)
- 1 cup BBQ sauce
- 4 tbsp pineapple juice
- ½ cup ketchup

Rub:

- 1 tsp garlic powder
- 1 tsp brown sugar
- 1 tsp dried peppermint
- 1 tsp onion powder
- 3 tsp paprika
- 2 tsp kosher salt
- ¼ tsp cayenne pepper

Directions:
1. To make rub, combine the garlic, sugar, peppermint, onion powder, paprika, salt and cayenne.
2. Rinse the chicken halves in cold running water. Pat chicken halves dry with paper towel.
3. Generously season all sides of the chicken halves with rub mix.
4. Configure your pellet grill for indirect heat and preheat to 225°F, using apple hardwood pellets.
5. Place chicken halves on the grill and cook for 2 hour or until the internal temperature of the chicken halves reaches 160°F.
6. Remove the chicken half from heat and let them cool for a few minutes.
7. Transfer chicken to a large bowl and shred with 2 forks.

8. Combine the ketchup, BBQ sauce and juice in a large saucepan over medium to high heat. Bring to a boil, reduce the heat and simmer until sauce thicken.
9. Stir in the shredded chicken and cook for about 5 minutes, stirring often to prevent burning.
10. Serve.

Nutrition Facts
Servings: 4

Amount per serving
Calories 790

% Daily Value*

Total Fat 25.7g	33%
Saturated Fat 7g	35%
Cholesterol 303mg	101%
Sodium 2491mg	108%
Total Carbohydrate 34.9g	13%
Dietary Fiber 1.3g	4%
Total Sugars 26g	
Protein 99.4g	
Vitamin D 0mcg	0%
Calcium 74mg	6%

Nutrition Facts
Servings: 4

Iron 5mg	28%
Potassium 1148mg	24%

Smoked Chicken Drumsticks

PREP TIME: 10 minutes
COOK TIME: 2 hours 30 minutes
SERVINGS: 5
Ingredients:
- 10 chicken drumsticks
- 2 tsp garlic powder

- 1 tsp salt
- 1 tsp onion powder
- 1/2 tsp ground black pepper
- ½ tsp cayenne pepper
- 1 tsp brown sugar
- 1/3 cup hot sauce
- 1 tsp paprika
- ½ tsp thyme

Directions:
1. In a mixing large bowl, combine the garlic powder, sugar, hit sauce, paprika, thyme, cayenne, salt and ground pepper. Add the drumsticks and toss to combine.
2. Cover the bowl and refrigerate for 1 hour.
3. Remove the drumsticks from the marinade and let them sit for about 1 hour, until they are at room temperature.
4. Arrange the drumsticks into a rack.
5. Start your pellet grill on smoke, leaving the lid opened for 5 minutes for fire to start.
6. Close the lid and preheat grill to 250°F, using hickory or apple hardwood pellets.
7. Place the rack on the grill and smoke drumsticks for 2 hours 30 minutes, or until the internal temperature of the drumsticks reaches 180°F

8. Remove drumsticks from heat and let them rest for a few minutes.
9. Serve.

Nutrition Facts

Servings: 5

Amount per serving

Calories 167

	% Daily Value*
Total Fat 5.4g	7%
Saturated Fat 1.4g	7%
Cholesterol 81mg	27%
Sodium 946mg	41%
Total Carbohydrate 2.6g	1%
Dietary Fiber 0.5g	2%
Total Sugars 1.3g	
Protein 25.7g	
Vitamin D 0mcg	0%
Calcium 19mg	1%
Iron 2mg	9%
Potassium 240mg	5%

Chicken Cordon Bleu

PREP TIME: 15 minutes
COOK TIME: 40 minutes
SERVINGS: 6
Ingredients:
- 6 boneless skinless chicken breasts
- 6 slices of ham
- 12 slices swiss cheese

- 1 cup panko breadcrumbs
- ½ cup all-purpose flour
- 1 tsp ground black pepper or to taste
- 1 tsp salt or to taste
- 4 tbsp grated parmesan cheese
- 2 tbsp melted butter
- ½ tsp garlic powder
- ½ tsp thyme
- ¼ tsp parsley

Directions:
1. Butterfly the chicken breast with a pairing knife. Place the chicken breast in between 2 plastic wraps and pound with a mallet until the chicken breasts are ¼ inch thick.
2. Place a plastic wrap on a flat surface. Place one fat chicken breast on it.
3. Place one slice of swiss cheese on the chicken. Place one slice of ham over the cheese and place another cheese slice over the ham.
4. Roll the chicken breast tightly. Fold both ends of the roll tightly. Pin both ends of the rolled chicken breast with toothpick.
5. Repeat step 3 and 4 for the remaining chicken breasts

6. In a mixing bowl, combine the all-purpose flour, ½ tsp salt and ½ tsp pepper. Set aside.
7. In another mixing bowl, combine breadcrumbs, parmesan, butter, garlic, thyme, parsley, ½ tsp salt and ½ tsp pepper. Set aside.
8. Break the eggs into another mixing bowl and whisk. Set aside.
9. Grease a baking sheet.
10. Take one chicken breast roll. Dip into the flour mixture, brush with eggs and dip into breadcrumb mixture. The chicken breast should be coated.
11. Place it on the baking sheet.
12. Repeat step 9 and 10 for the remaining breast rolls.
13. Preheat your grill to 375°F with lid closed for 15 minutes.
14. Place the baking sheet on the grill and cook for about 40 minutes, or until the chicken is golden brown.
15. Remove baking sheet from the grill and let the chicken rest for a few minutes.
16. Slice cordon bleu and serve.

Nutrition Facts
Servings: 6

Amount per serving
Calories 560

	% Daily Value*
Total Fat 27.4g	35%
Saturated Fat 15.9g	80%
Cholesterol 156mg	52%
Sodium 1158mg	50%
Total Carbohydrate 23.2g	8%
Dietary Fiber 1.1g	4%
Total Sugars 1.2g	
Protein 54.3g	
Vitamin D 27mcg	136%
Calcium 623mg	48%
Iron 2mg	10%
Potassium 144mg	3%

Smoked Whole Duck

PREP TIME: 15 minutes
COOK TIME: 2 hours 30 minutes
SERVINGS: 6
Ingredients:
- 5 pounds whole duck (trimmed of any excess fat)
- 1 small onion (quartered)
- 1 apple (wedged)
- 1 orange (quartered)
- 1 tbsp freshy chopped parsley
- 1 tbsp freshly chopped sage

- ½ tsp onion powder
- 2 tsp smoked paprika
- 1 tsp dried Italian seasoning
- 1 tbsp dried Greek seasoning
- 1 tsp pepper or to taste
- 1 tsp sea salt or to taste

Directions:
1. Remove giblets and rinse duck, inside and pour, under cold running water.
2. Pat dry with paper towels.
3. Use the tip of a sharp knife to cut the duck skin all over. Be careful not to cut through the meat. Tie the duck legs together with butcher's string.
4. To make rub, combine the onion powder, pepper, salt, Italian seasoning, Greek seasoning and paprika in a mixing bowl.
5. Insert the orange, onion and apple to the duck cavity. Stuff the duck with freshly chopped parsley and sage.
6. Season all sides of the duck generously with rub mixture.
7. Start your pellet grill on smoke mode, leaving the lip opened or until fire starts.
8. Close the lid and preheat grill to 325°F for 10 minutes.

9. Place the duck on the grill grate.
10. Roast for 2 to 21/2 hours, or until the duck skin is brown and the internal temperature of the thigh reaches 160°F.
11. Remove the duck from heat and let it rest for a few minutes.
12. Cut into sizes and serve.

Nutrition Facts

Servings: 6

Amount per serving

Calories 809

% Daily Value*

Total Fat 42.9g	55%
Saturated Fat 15.8g	79%
Cholesterol 337mg	112%
Sodium 638mg	28%
Total Carbohydrate 11.7g	4%
Dietary Fiber 2.4g	9%
Total Sugars 7.5g	
Protein 89.6g	
Vitamin D 0mcg	0%
Calcium 70mg	5%
Iron 11mg	60%

Nutrition Facts
Servings: 6

Potassium 1104mg　　　　　　　　　23%

Chicken Tenders

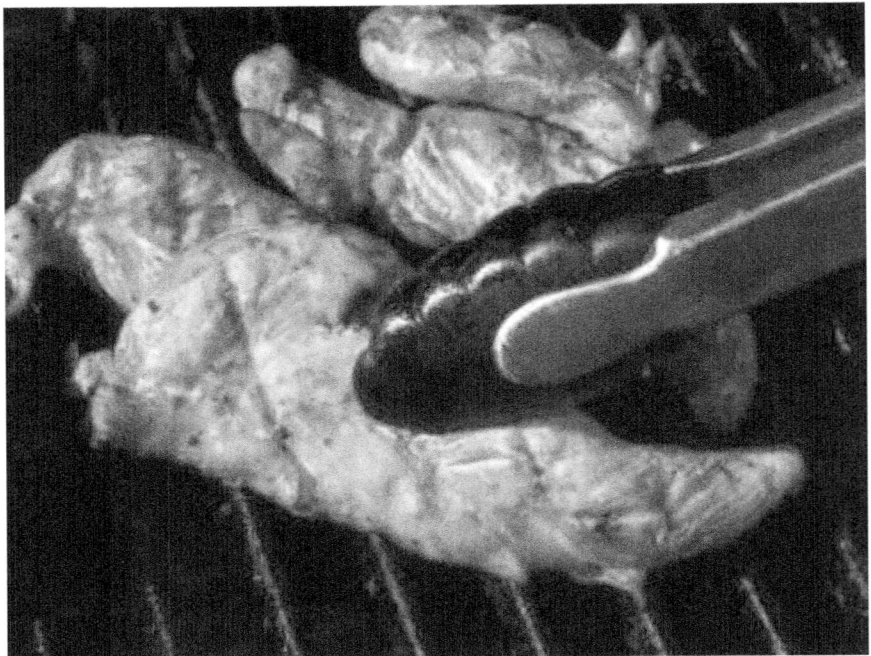

PREP TIME: 10 minutes
COOK TIME: 8 minutes
SERVINGS: 6
Ingredients:
- 6 chicken tenders
- ¼ tsp granulated garlic (not garlic powder)
- ¼ tsp pepper

- 1 tsp paprika
- ½ tsp kosher salt
- 1 tbsp olive oil
- `1 tbsp lemon juice
- 1 tsp Italian seasoning
- 1 tbsp chopped parsley

Directions:
1. In a large mixing bowl, combine the garlic, pepper, salt, lemon, Italian seasoning and paprika. Add the chicken tenders and toss to combine. Cover the bowl and refrigerate for 1 hour.
2. Remove the chicken tenders from the marinade and let them rest for 1 hour, until the tenders are at room temperature. Pat dry with paper towels.
3. Configure your grill for direct smoking and preheat grill to 450°F.
4. Arrange the chicken tenders onto the grill and grill 8 minutes, 4 minutes per side.
5. Remove the tenders from the grill.
6. Serve and garnish with chopped fresh parsley.

Nutrition Facts
Servings: 6

Amount per serving
Calories 459

	% Daily Value*
Total Fat 23.6g	30%
Saturated Fat 4g	20%
Cholesterol 49mg	16%
Sodium 1556mg	68%
Total Carbohydrate 32.9g	12%
Dietary Fiber 2.6g	9%
Total Sugars 0.2g	
Protein 28.9g	
Vitamin D 0mcg	0%
Calcium 2mg	0%
Iron 0mg	1%
Potassium 18mg	0%

Thanksgiving Turkey

PREP TIME: 15 minutes
COOK TIME: 4 hours
SERVINGS: 12
Ingredients:
- 2 cups butter (softened)
- 1 tbsp cracked black pepper
- 2 tsp kosher salt
- 2 tbsp freshly chopped rosemary
- 2 tbsp freshly chopped parsley
- 2 tbsp freshly chopped sage
- 2 tsp dried thyme

- 6 garlic cloves (minced)
- 1 (18 pound) turkey

Directions:
1. In a mixing bowl, combine the butter, sage, rosemary, 1 tsp black pepper, 1 tsp salt, thyme, parsley and garlic.
2. Use your fingers to loosen the skin from the turkey.
3. Generously, Rub butter mixture under the turkey skin and all over the turkey as well.
4. Season turkey generously with herb mix.
5. Preheat the grill to 300°F with lid closed for 15 minutes.
6. Place the turkey on the grill and roast for about 4 hours, or until the turkey thigh temperature reaches 160°F.
7. Remove the turkey from the grill and let it rest for a few minutes.
8. Cut into sizes and serve.

Nutrition Facts

Servings: 12

Amount per serving	
Calories	**278**
	% Daily Value*
Total Fat 30.8g	40%

Nutrition Facts

Servings: 12

Saturated Fat 19.5g	**98%**
Cholesterol 81mg	**27%**
Sodium 608mg	**26%**
Total Carbohydrate 1.6g	**1%**
Dietary Fiber 0.6g	**2%**
Total Sugars 0.1g	
Protein 0.6g	
Vitamin D 21mcg	106%
Calcium 31mg	2%
Iron 1mg	4%
Potassium 36mg	1%

Spatchcock Smoked Turkey

PREP TIME: 15 minutes
COOK TIME: 4 hours 30 minutes
SERVINGS: 12
Ingredients:
- 1 (18 pounds) turkey
- 2 tbsp finely chopped fresh parsley
- 1 tbsp finely chopped fresh rosemary
- 2 tbsp finely chopped fresh thyme
- ½ cup melted butter
- 1 tsp garlic powder
- 1 tsp onion powder

- 1 tsp ground black pepper
- 2 tsp salt or to taste
- 2 tbsp finely chopped scallions

Directions:
1. Remove the turkey giblets and rinse turkey, in and out, under cold running water.
2. Place the turkey on a working surface, breast side down. Use a poultry shear to cut the turkey along both sides of the backbone to remove the turkey back bone.
3. Flip the turkey over, back side down. Now, press the turkey down to flatten it.
4. In a mixing bowl, combine the parsley, rosemary, scallions, thyme, butter, pepper, salt, garlic and onion powder.
5. Rub butter mixture over all sides of the turkey.
6. Preheat your grill to HIGH (450°F) with lid closed for 15 minutes.
7. Place the turkey directly on the grill grate and cook for 30 minutes. Reduce the heat to 300°F and cook for an additional 4 hours, or until the internal temperature of the thickest part of the thigh reaches 165°F.
8. Remove the turkey from the grill and let it rest for a few minutes.

9. Cut into sizes and serve.

Nutrition Facts
Servings: 12

Amount per serving
Calories 780

	% Daily Value*
Total Fat 19g	**24%**
Saturated Fat 7.2g	**36%**
Cholesterol 313mg	**104%**
Sodium 7349mg	**320%**
Total Carbohydrate 29.7g	**11%**
Dietary Fiber 3.8g	**14%**
Total Sugars 24.1g	
Protein 116.4g	
Vitamin D 5mcg	27%
Calcium 72mg	6%
Iron 11mg	59%
Potassium 2076mg	44%

Smoked Chicken Leg Quarters

PREP TIME: 15 minutes
COOK TIME: 2 hours
SERVINGS: 8
Ingredients:
- 8 chicken leg quarters
- 2 tbsp olive oil
- 1 tsp salt or to taste
- ½ tsp chili powder
- ½ tsp paprika

- ½ tsp ground thyme
- 1 tsp dried rosemary
- ½ tsp cayenne pepper
- 1 tsp garlic powder
- 1 tsp onion powder

Directions:
1. To make rub, combine cayenne, rosemary, garlic, onion powder, chili, paprika, salt and thyme.
2. Drizzle oil over the chicken leg quarters and season the quarters generously with rub mix.
3. Preheat the grill to 180°F with lid closed for 15 minutes, using apple hardwood pellets.
4. Arrange the chicken onto the grill grate. Smoke for 1 hour, flipping half way through.
5. Increase the grill temperature to 350°F. Cook for an additional 1 hour, or until the temperature of the chicken quarters reaches 165°F.
6. Remove chicken from grill and let it rest for about 15 minutes.
7. Serve and enjoy.

Nutrition Facts

Servings: 8

Amount per serving

Calories 34

	% Daily Value*
Total Fat 3.6g	5%
Saturated Fat 0.5g	3%
Cholesterol 0mg	0%
Sodium 293mg	13%
Total Carbohydrate 0.9g	0%
Dietary Fiber 0.3g	1%
Total Sugars 0.2g	
Protein 0.2g	
Vitamin D 0mcg	0%
Calcium 5mg	0%
Iron 0mg	1%
Potassium 17mg	0%

Chicken Fajitas

PREP TIME: 10 minutes
COOK TIME: 20 minutes
SERVINGS: 4
Ingredients:
- 2 pounds chicken breast
- 1 large onion (sliced)
- 2 celery stalks (diced)
- 1 large red bell pepper (sliced)
- 1 large orange bell pepper (sliced)
- 1 green bell pepper (sliced)
- 2 tbsp lime juice

- 2 tsp cumin
- 2 tsp chili powder
- 1 tsp brown sugar
- ½ tsp paprika
- 1 tbsp olive oil
- 1 tsp salt
- ½ tsp ground black pepper

Directions:
1. In a large mixing bowl, combine the cumin, lime juice, salt, black pepper, paprika and sugar. Add the chicken breasts and toss to combine. Cover the bowl tightly with aluminum foil and refrigerate for 1 hour.
2. Remove the chicken from the marinade and let it rest for about 1 hour, or until it is at room temperature.
3. Preheat your grill to HIGH with lid closed for 15 minutes.
4. Place a skillet on the grill grate and add the oil.
5. Once the oil is hot, add the onion, celery, red bell pepper, orange pepper and green bell pepper. Saute until veggies are tender.
6. Remove skillet from heat and cover it to keep the veggies warm.

7. Arrange the chicken breasts onto the grill grate. Cook for about 12 minutes, 6 minutes per side, or until the internal temperature of the chicken breasts reaches 165°F.
8. Remove the chicken from heat and let it rest for a few minutes.
9. Slice chicken breast into thin pieces.
10. Serve with the sautéed vegetables and tortilla.

Nutrition Facts
Servings: 4

Amount per serving
Calories 346

	% Daily Value*
Total Fat 9.9g	13%
Saturated Fat 0.6g	3%
Cholesterol 145mg	48%
Sodium 723mg	31%
Total Carbohydrate 13.2g	5%
Dietary Fiber 3.1g	11%
Total Sugars 6.4g	
Protein 49.9g	
Vitamin D 0mcg	1%

Nutrition Facts
Servings: 4

Calcium 48mg	4%
Iron 2mg	12%
Potassium 1104mg	23%

Grilled Chicken Kebabs

PREP TIME: 15 minutes
COOK TIME: 12 minutes
SERVINGS: 6
Ingredients:

- 1 ½ pounds boneless skinless chicken thighs (Cut into 2-inch cubes)
- 1 large bell pepper (sliced)
- 1 large yellow bell pepper (sliced)
- 1 large green bell pepper (sliced)
- 1 onion (sliced)
- 10 medium cremini mushrooms (destemmed and halved)
- Wooden or bamboo skewers (soaked in water for 30 minutes, at least)

Marinade:
- 2 tbsp honey
- 1 tsp Italian seasoning
- 2 tbsp finely chopped fresh parsley
- 2 tsp finely chopped fresh thyme
- ½ tsp ground black pepper
- ½ cup olive oil
- ½ tsp salt or to taste
- 1 lemon (juiced)
- ½ tsp cayenne pepper

Directions:
1. In a large mixing bowl, combine all the marinade ingredients. Add the chicken and mushroom. Toss to combine. Cover the bowl tightly with aluminum foil and refrigerate for 45 minutes.

2. Remove the mushroom and chicken from the marinade.
3. Thread the bell peppers, onion, mushroom and chicken unto skewers to make kabobs.
4. Preheat your grill to HIGH with lid closed for 15 minutes, using mesquite hardwood pellets.
5. Arrange the kebobs onto the grill grate and grill for 12 minutes, 6 minutes per side.
6. Remove kebabs from heat.
7. Serve warm and enjoy.

Nutrition Facts

Servings: 6

Amount per serving

Calories   **419**

                          % Daily Value*

Total Fat 25.7g   33%

  Saturated Fat 4.8g   24%

Cholesterol 101mg   34%

Sodium 303mg   13%

Total Carbohydrate 13.8g   5%

  Dietary Fiber 2.1g   7%

  Total Sugars 9.6g

Protein 34.6g

Nutrition Facts
Servings: 6

Vitamin D 0mcg	0%
Calcium 46mg	4%
Iron 2mg	14%
Potassium 581mg	12%

Chicken Enchiladas

PREP TIME: 15 minutes
COOK TIME: 45 minutes
SERVINGS: 6

Ingredients:
- 2 pounds shredded chicken
- 1 tbsp olive oil
- ½ tbsp taco seasoning
- 1 tsp salt
- 1 tsp onion powder
- 1 tsp ground black pepper
- ½ tsp garlic powder
- 1 can (28 ounces) enchilada sauce
- 1 onion (diced)
- 2 cups Mexican blend shredded cheese
- 8 large flour tortilla
- 1 cup sour cream
- 1 (7 ounces) diced green chiles
- 2 tbsp cilantro (chopped)

Directions:
1. In a large mixing bowl, combine the shredded chicken, sour cream, onion, 1 cup shredded cheese, green chiles, onion powder, taco seasoning, pepper and garlic powder.
2. Spoon equal amount of the chicken mixture into each tortilla and roll.
3. Arrange the stuffed tortilla into a 9-inch by 13-iinch greased baking pan. Pour the enchilada sauce over the tortilla and top

with the remaining 1 cup cheese. Cover the pan tightly with aluminum foil.
4. Preheat your grill to 350°F with lid closed for 15 minutes, using mesquite hardwood pellets.
5. Place the pan on the grill and cook for 30 minutes.
6. Uncover the pan and cook for an additional 1 hour.
7. Remove pan from heat and let the enchilada rest for a few minutes.
8. Cut into sizes. Serve and garnish with chopped cilantro.

Nutrition Facts

Servings: 6

Amount per serving

Calories — **546**

	% Daily Value*
Total Fat 25.3g	32%
Saturated Fat 12.8g	64%
Cholesterol 160mg	53%
Sodium 1136mg	49%
Total Carbohydrate 22.6g	8%
Dietary Fiber 2.6g	9%

Nutrition Facts
Servings: 6

Total Sugars 4g

Protein 55.2g

Vitamin D 0mcg	0%
Calcium 365mg	28%
Iron 2mg	11%
Potassium 446mg	9%

Hoisin Turkey Wings

PREP TIME: 15 minutes
COOK TIME: 1 hour 6 minutes
SERVINGS: 8

Ingredients:
- 2 pounds turkey wings
- ½ cup hoisin sauce
- 1 tbsp honey
- 2 tsp soy sauce
- 2 garlic cloves (minced)
- 1 tsp freshly grated ginger
- 2 tsp sesame oil
- 1 tsp pepper or to taste
- 1 tsp salt or to taste
- ¼ cup pineapple juice
- 1 tbsp chopped green onions
- 1 tbsp sesame seeds
- 1 lemon (cut into wedges)

Directions:
1. In a large mixing bowl, combine the honey, garlic, ginger, soy, hoisin sauce, sesame oil, pepper and salt. Pour the mixture into a ziplock bag and add the wings. Refrigerate for 2 hours.
2. Remove turkey from the marinade and reserve the marinade. Let the turkey rest for a few minutes, until it is at room temperature.

3. Preheat your grill to 300°F with the lid closed for 15 minutes.
4. Arrange the wings into a grilling basket and place the basket on the grill.
5. Grill for 1 hour or until the internal temperature of the wings reaches 165°F.
6. Meanwhile, pour the reserved marinade into a saucepan over medium-high heat. Stir in the pineapple juice.
7. Bring to a boil, reduce heat and simmer for until the sauce thickens.
8. Brush the wings with sauce and cook for 6 minutes more.
9. Remove the wings from heat.
10. Serve and top with green onions, sesame seeds and lemon wedges.

Nutrition Facts

Servings: 8

Amount per serving

Calories 115

% Daily Value*

Total Fat 4.8g	6%
Saturated Fat 0.3g	2%
Cholesterol 0mg	0%
Sodium 625mg	27%

Nutrition Facts
Servings: 8

Total Carbohydrate 11.9g	**4%**
Dietary Fiber 1g	**3%**
Total Sugars 7.5g	
Protein 6.8g	
Vitamin D 0mcg	0%
Calcium 23mg	2%
Iron 1mg	3%
Potassium 60mg	1%

Turkey Jerky

PREP TIME: 15 minutes
COOK TIME: 4 hours
SERVINGS: 10
Ingredients:
Marinade:
- 1 cup pineapple juice
- ½ cup brown sugar
- 2 tbsp sriracha
- 2 tsp onion powder
- 2 tbsp minced garlic
- 2 tbsp rice wine vinegar

- 2 tbsp hoison
- 1 tbsp red pepper flakes
- 1 tbsp coarsely ground black pepper flakes
- 2 cups coconut aminos
- 2 jalapenos (thinly sliced)

Meat:
- 3 pounds turkey boneless skinless breasts (sliced to ¼ inch thick)

Directions:
10. Combine all the marinade ingredients in a mixing bowl and mix until the ingredients are well combined.
11. Put the turkey slices in a gallon sized zip-lock bag and pour the marinade into the bag. Massage the marinade into the turkey. Seal the bag and refrigerate for 8 hours.
12. Remove the turkey slices from the marinade.
13. Activate the pellet grill for smoking and leave lip opened for 5 minutes until fire starts.
14. Close the lid and preheat your pellet grill to 180°F, using hickory pellet.
15. Remove the turkey slices from the marinade and pat them dry with a paper towel.

16. Arrange the turkey slices on the grill in a single layer. Smoke the turkey for about 3 to 4 hours, turning often after the first 2 hours of smoking. The jerky should be dark and dry when it is done.
17. Remove the jerky from the grill and let it sit for about 1 hour to cool.
18. Serve immediately or store in refrigerator.

Honey Baked Mustard Chicken

PREP TIME: 15 minutes
COOK TIME: 35 minutes
SERVINGS: 4
Ingredients:
- 4 boneless skinless chicken breasts (4 ounces each)
- 1 tbsp grainy mustard

- 4 tbsp honey
- ½ tsp white vinegar
- ½ tsp paprika
- 2 tbsp Dijon mustard
- 1 tbsp + 2 tsp olive oil
- 1 tsp salt
- 1 tsp ground black pepper or to taste
- 1 tbsp freshly chopped parsley
- 1 tsp dried basil

Directions:
1. Preheat the wood pellet grill to 375°F with lid closed for 15 minutes.
2. Grease a baking dish with a non-sticky cooking spray.
3. Season both sides of the chicken breasts with pepper and salt.
4. Place a cast iron skillet on the grill and add 2 tsp olive oil.
5. Once the oil is hot, add the seasoned chicken breast and sauté until both sides of the chicken breasts are browned.
6. Use a slotted spoon to transfer the fried chicken breast to a paper towel lined plate.
7. Combine the Dijon mustard, honey, vinegar, basil, grainy mustard, remaining oil and paprika in a mixing bowl. Mix until the ingredients are well combined.

8. Pour half of the honey mixture into the prepared baking dish and spread it to cover the bottom of the dish.
9. Arrange the chicken breast into the dish and pour the remaining honey mixture over the chicken.
10. Cover the baking dish with foil and place it on the grill. Cook on grill for about 20 minutes.
11. Remove the foil cover and cook, uncovered, for additional 15 minutes.
12. Remove the baking dish from the grill and let the chicken cool for a few minutes.
13. Serve and enjoy.

Nutrition Facts
Servings: 4

Amount per serving	
Calories	**320**
	% Daily Value*
Total Fat 12.4g	**16%**
Saturated Fat 2.9g	**14%**
Cholesterol 101mg	**34%**
Sodium 786mg	**34%**
Total Carbohydrate 18.5g	**7%**
Dietary Fiber 0.6g	**2%**
Total Sugars 17.4g	

Nutrition Facts
Servings: 4

Protein 33.4g

Vitamin D 0mcg	0%
Calcium 28mg	2%
Iron 2mg	10%
Potassium 317mg	7%

Chicken Nuggets

PREP TIME: 15 minutes
COOK TIME: 16 minutes
SERVINGS: 2
Ingredients:
- 4-ounce boneless skinless chicken breast (cut into bite sizes)
- ½ tsp salt or to taste

- ½ cup bread crumbs
- ¼ tsp sugar
- 2 tbsp buttermilk
- ½ lemon (squeezed)
- ½ tsp garlic powder
- ¼ ground black pepper
- ¼ tsp nutmeg
- A pinch of Italian seasoning

Directions:
1. Combine the chicken, sugar buttermilk and lemon in a bowl. Toss until well combined. Place the bowl in a refrigerator and marinate for about 2 hours.
2. Start your grill on smoke mode, leaving the lid opened for 5 minutes or until fire starts.
3. Close the lid and preheat the grill to 400°F for 5 minutes, using hickory hardwood pellet.
4. Grease a baking pan with non-stick spray.
5. Put the breadcrumbs in a bowl. Set aside.
6. Mix the pepper, salt, Italian seasoning and nutmeg in another bowl. Set aside.
7. Remove the chicken slices from the marinade and season with the seasoning mixture.

8. Dip each chicken piece into the breadcrumbs. Make sure all sides of each chicken piece are coated with breadcrumbs.
9. Arrange the coated chicken into the baking pan and press the chicken pieces to flatten them.
10. Place the baking pan directly on the grill and bake for 16 minutes or until chicken pieces turn golden brown.
11. Remove the chicken from the grill and let them cool for a few minutes.
12. Serve

Nutrition Facts
Servings: 2

Amount per serving	
Calories	**231**
	% Daily Value*
Total Fat 6g	8%
Saturated Fat 1.7g	8%
Cholesterol 51mg	17%
Sodium 844mg	37%
Total Carbohydrate 22.7g	8%
Dietary Fiber 1.8g	6%
Total Sugars 3.5g	

Nutrition Facts
Servings: 2

Protein 20.8g

Vitamin D 0mcg	0%
Calcium 81mg	6%
Iron 2mg	12%
Potassium 243mg	5%

Chapter Three

Pork Recipes

Pork Burnt Ends

PREP TIME: 15 minutes
COOK TIME: 4 hours 30 minutes
SERVINGS: 10
Ingredients:
- 4 pounds pork belly
- 4 tbsp brown sugar

- ¼ tsp cayenne pepper
- 1 tsp red pepper flakes
- ½ tsp onion powder
- ½ tsp garlic powder
- 1 tbsp paprika
- 1 tsp oregano
- 1 tbsp freshly ground black pepper
- 2 tbsp salt or to taste
- 1 tsp dried peppermint
- 2 tbsp olive oil
- ¼ cup butter
- 1 cup BBQ sauce
- 4 tbsp maple syrup
- 2 tbsp chopped fresh parsley

Directions:
1. Trim pork belly of any excess fat and cut off silver skin. Cut the pork into ½ inch cubes.
2. To make rub, combine the sugar, cayenne, pepper flakes, onion powder, garlic, paprika, oregano, black pepper, salt and peppermint in a mixing bowl.
3. Drizzle oil over the pork and season each pork cubes generously with the rub.
4. Preheat your grill to 205°F with lid closed for 15 minutes.

5. Arrange the pork chunks onto the grill grate and smoke for about 3 hours, or until the pork chunks turn dark red.
6. Meanwhile, combine the BBQ sauce, maple syrup and butter in an aluminum pan.
7. Remove the pork slices from heat and put them in the pan, with the sauce. Stir to combine.
8. Cover the pan tightly with aluminum foil and place it on the grill. Cook for 1 hour or until the internal temperature of the pork reaches 200°F.
9. Remove the pork from heat and let it sit for some minutes.
10. Serve and garnish with fresh chopped parsley.

Nutrition Facts

Servings: 10

Amount per serving

Calories 477

	% Daily Value*
Total Fat 41.8g	54%
Saturated Fat 15.8g	79%
Cholesterol 58mg	19%
Sodium 1747mg	76%

Nutrition Facts
Servings: 10

Total Carbohydrate 19.3g	**7%**
Dietary Fiber 0.7g	**3%**
Total Sugars 15.1g	
Protein 6.4g	
Vitamin D 3mcg	16%
Calcium 22mg	2%
Iron 1mg	6%
Potassium 110mg	2%

Pork Prime Rib

PREP TIME: 10 minutes
COOK TIME: 2 hours
SERVINGS: 12
Ingredients:
- 6 pounds prime pork rib
- 1 tbsp salt
- 1 tbsp ground black pepper

Wet Rub:
- 1 cup Dijon mustard
- 2 tsp sea salt
- 2 tbsp ground black pepper

- 1 tbsp finely chopped fresh rosemary
- 1 tsp dried thyme
- 1 tsp garlic powder
- ½ tsp paprika
- 1 tsp onion powder
- 2 tbsp soy sauce
- 1 tbsp Worcestershire sauce
- 1 tbsp red wine vinegar

Directions:
1. Season all sides of the pork with salt and pepper.
2. In a mixing bowl, combine all the ingredients for a wet rub.
3. Liberally rub the mixture over all part of the pork.
4. Configure your pellet grill for indirect cooking and preheat the grill to 300°F.
5. Place the pork rib on the grill grate and cook for about 2 hours, or until the internal temperature of the rib reaches 140°F.
6. Remove the pork from the heat and let it rest for a few minutes.
7. Cut into sizes and serve.

Nutrition Facts

Servings: 12

Amount per serving

Calories 382

% Daily Value*

Total Fat 19g	24%
Saturated Fat 6.1g	31%
Cholesterol 151mg	50%
Sodium 1445mg	63%
Total Carbohydrate 2.5g	1%
Dietary Fiber 1.1g	4%
Total Sugars 0.6g	
Protein 45.4g	
Vitamin D 0mcg	0%
Calcium 62mg	5%
Iron 3mg	16%
Potassium 52mg	1%

Grilled Carnitas

PREP TIME: 20 minutes
COOK TIME: 10 hours
SERVINGS: 12
Ingredients:
- 1 tsp paprika
- 1 tsp oregano
- 1 tsp cayenne pepper
- 2 tsp brown sugar
- 1 tsp mint
- 1 tbsp onion powder

- 1 tsp cumin
- 1 tsp chili powder
- 2 tbsp salt
- 1 tsp garlic powder
- 1 tsp Italian seasoning
- 2 tbsp olive oil.
- 5 pounds pork shoulder roast

Directions:
1. Trim the pork of any excess fat.
2. To make rub, combine the paprika, oregano, cayenne, sugar, mint, onion powder, garlic powder, cumin, chili, salt and Italian seasoning in a small mixing bowl.
3. Liberally, rub all sides of the pork with the rub.
4. Start your grill for smoking, leaving the lid opened until fire starts.
5. Close the lid and preheat grill to 325°F with lid closed for 15 minutes.
6. Place the pork in a foil pan and place the pan on the grill. Cook for about 2 hours.
7. After 2 hours, increase the heat to 325°F and smoke pork for an additional 8 hours or until the internal temperature of the pork reaches 190°F.

8. Remove pork from it and let it sit until it is cook and easy to handle.
9. Shred the pork with two forks.
10. Place a cast iron skillet on the grill grate and add the olive oil.
11. Add the pork and sear until the pork is brown and crispy.
12. Remove pork from heat and let it rest for a few minutes.
13. Serve.

Nutrition Facts

Servings: 12

Amount per serving

Calories 514

	% Daily Value*
Total Fat 41.1g	53%
Saturated Fat 13.7g	69%
Cholesterol 134mg	45%
Sodium 1292mg	56%
Total Carbohydrate 1.6g	1%
Dietary Fiber 0.3g	1%
Total Sugars 0.9g	
Protein 32g	

Nutrition Facts
Servings: 12

Vitamin D 0mcg	0%
Calcium 9mg	1%
Iron 2mg	12%
Potassium 27mg	1%

Stuffed Tenderloin

PREP TIME: 15 minutes
COOK TIME: 3 hours
SERVINGS: 8
Ingredients:
- 1 pork tenderloin

- 12 slices of bacon
- ¼ cup cheddar cheese
- ¼ cup mozzarella cheese
- 1 small onion (finely chopped)
- 1 carrot (finely chopped)

Rub:
- ½ tsp granulated garlic (not garlic powder)
- ½ tsp cayenne pepper
- 1 tsp paprika
- ½ tsp ground pepper
- 1 tsp chili
- ½ tsp onion powder
- ¼ tsp cumin
- 1 tsp salt

Directions:
1. Butterfly the pork tenderloin and place between 2 plastic wraps. Pound the tenderloin evenly with a mallet until it is ½ inch thick.
2. Place the cheddar, mozzarella, onion and carrot on one end of the flat pork. Roll up the pork like a burrito.
3. Combine all the ingredients for the rub in a mixing bowl.
4. Generously, rub the seasoning mixture all the over the pork.

5. Wrap the pork with bacon slices.
6. Start your grill for smoking, leaving the lid open until fire starts.
7. Close the lid and preheat the grill to 275°F for 10-15 minutes. Use apple, hickory or mesquite hardwood pellets.
8. Place the pork on the grill and smoke for 3 hours, or until the internal temperature of the pork reaches 165°F and the bacon wrap is crispy.
9. Remove the pork from heat and let it rest for about 10 minutes.
10. Cut into sizes and serve.

Nutrition Facts

Servings: 8

Amount per serving

Calories 241

	% Daily Value*
Total Fat 14.8g	19%
Saturated Fat 5.3g	26%
Cholesterol 66mg	22%
Sodium 1010mg	44%
Total Carbohydrate 2.7g	1%
Dietary Fiber 0.6g	2%

Nutrition Facts
Servings: 8

Total Sugars 0.9g

Protein 22.9g

Vitamin D 0mcg	2%
Calcium 39mg	3%
Iron 1mg	6%
Potassium 394mg	8%

Pork Kebabs

PREP TIME: 10 minutes
COOK TIME: 12 minutes
SERVINGS: 4
Ingredients:
- 1 pork tenderloin (cut into 2-inch cubes)
- 1 large bell pepper (sliced)
- 1 large yellow bell pepper (sliced)
- 1 large green bell pepper (sliced)
- 1 onion (sliced)
- 10 medium cremini mushrooms (destemmed and halved)

- Wooden or bamboo skewers (soaked in water for 30 minutes, at least)

Marinade:
- ½ cup olive oil
- ½ tsp pepper
- 1 tsp salt
- 1 tbsp freshly chopped parsley
- 3 tbsp brown sugar
- 2 tsp Dijon mustard
- 3 tbsp soy sauce
- 1 lemon (juice)
- 1 tbsp freshly chopped thyme
- 1 tsp minced garlic

Directions:
8. In a large mixing bowl, combine all the marinade ingredients. Add the pork and mushroom. Toss to combine. Cover the bowl tightly with aluminum foil and refrigerate for 8 hours.
9. Remove the mushroom and pork from the marinade.
10. Thread the bell peppers, onion, mushroom and pork onto skewers to make kabobs.
11. Preheat your grill to HIGH with lid closed for 15 minutes, using mesquite hardwood pellets.

12. Arrange the kebobs onto the grill grate and grill for 12 minutes, 6 minutes per side, or until the internal temperature of the pork reaches 145°F.
13. Remove kebabs from heat.
14. Serve warm and enjoy.

Nutrition Facts
Servings: 8

Amount per serving
Calories 272

	% Daily Value*
Total Fat 15.8g	20%
Saturated Fat 2.8g	14%
Cholesterol 62mg	21%
Sodium 701mg	30%
Total Carbohydrate 9.2g	3%
Dietary Fiber 1.4g	5%
Total Sugars 6g	
Protein 24g	
Vitamin D 0mcg	0%
Calcium 31mg	2%
Iron 2mg	11%
Potassium 590mg	13%

Scotch Eggs

PREP TIME: 20 minutes
COOK TIME: 1 hour 30 minutes
SERVINGS: 6
Ingredients:

- 1 pound ground pork
- 6 large hard-boiled eggs (peeled)
- 1 tsp salt
- 1 tsp ground black pepper
- 1 tsp garlic powder
- ½ tsp chili

Rub:

- 2 tsp brown sugar

- ½ tsp salt
- 1 tsp mustard powder
- ½ tsp cayenne pepper
- 1 tsp paprika
- 1 tsp chili powder
- 1 tsp mustard powder

Directions:
1. In a small mixing bowl, combine all the rub ingredients. Set aside.
2. In a large mixing bowl, combine the pork, pepper, garlic, chili and salt. Mix until well combined.
3. Roll the pork mixture into 6 equal ball and place each ball on a waxed paper. Press each ball into a flat 4-inch wide circle.
4. Place one egg on one flat pork portion and wrap the egg with the pork mixture. The pork mixture should cover the egg completely.
5. Repeat step 4 to make the remaining 5 scotch eggs.
6. Rub egg scotch egg generously with the rub mixture.
7. Arrange the scotch eggs into a wax paper lined baking pan. Refrigerate for 1 hour.

8. When ready to smoke, configure your grill for indirect cooking and preheat the grill to 235°F.
9. Arrange the scotch eggs on to the grill grate. Cook for about 1 ½ hours, or until the back of the scotch egg turns golden brown and crispy.
10. Remove the scotch egg from it and let it rest for few minutes.
11. Half scotch eggs and serve.

Nutrition Facts
Servings: 6

Amount per serving
Calories 195

	% Daily Value*
Total Fat 8.1g	10%
Saturated Fat 2.5g	13%
Cholesterol 241mg	80%
Sodium 702mg	31%
Total Carbohydrate 3g	1%
Dietary Fiber 0.7g	2%
Total Sugars 1.7g	
Protein 26.6g	

Nutrition Facts
Servings: 6

Vitamin D 18mcg	88%
Calcium 43mg	3%
Iron 2mg	12%
Potassium 427mg	9%

Maplewood Bourbon BBQ Ham

PREP TIME: 15 minutes

COOK TIME: 2 hours 30 minutes
SERVINGS: 8
Ingredients:
- 1 large ham
- 1/2 cup brown sugar
- 3 tbsp bourbon
- 2 tbsp lemon
- 2 tbsp Dijon mustard
- ¼ cup apple juice
- ¼ cup maple syrup
- 1 tsp salt
- 1 tsp freshly ground garlic
- 1 tsp ground black pepper

Directions:
1. Start your grill on smoke setting, leaving the opened for 5 minutes, until fire starts.
2. Close the lid and preheat grill to 325°F.
3. Place the ham on a smoker rack and place the rack on the grill. Smoke for 2 hours or until the internal temperature of the ham reaches 125°F.
4. Meanwhile, combine the sugar, bourbon, lemon, mustard, apple juice, salt, pepper and maple in a saucepan over medium to high eat.
5. Bring mixture to a boil, reduce the heat and simmer until the sauce thickens.

6. Glaze the ham with maple mixture.
7. Increase the grill temperature to 375°F and continue cooking until the internal temperature of the ham reaches 140°F.
8. Remove the glaze ham from the grill and let it rest for about 15 minutes.
9. Cut ham into small sizes and serve.

Nutrition Facts

Servings: 8

Amount per serving

Calories 163

% Daily Value*

Total Fat 4.6g	6%
Saturated Fat 1.5g	8%
Cholesterol 29mg	10%
Sodium 999mg	43%
Total Carbohydrate 19g	7%
Dietary Fiber 1g	3%
Total Sugars 15.5g	
Protein 8.7g	
Vitamin D 0mcg	0%
Calcium 31mg	2%
Iron 1mg	5%

Nutrition Facts
Servings: 8

Potassium 199mg   4%

Country Style Pork Ribs

PREP TIME: 15 minutes
COOK TIME: 3 hours 20 minutes
SERVINGS: 8
Ingredients:
- 4 pounds country-style pork ribs
- 1 cup BBQ sauce

Braise ingredients:
- ¾ cup cider vinegar
- 1 ½ cup apple juice
- 1 tsp ground black pepper
- 1 tsp paprika
- 1 tsp dried basil
- 1 tsp dried oregano
- 1 tsp dried thyme
- 2 tsp brown sugar
- 1 tsp mustard powder

Rub:
- 1 tbsp brown sugar
- 2 tsp kosher salt
- 1 tsp poultry seasoning
- 1 tsp cayenne pepper
- 1 tsp ground black pepper
- 1 tsp onion powder
- ½ tsp paprika
- ½ tsp red pepper flakes

Directions:
1. Combine all the rub ingredients in a large mixing bowl. Add the pork ribs and toss to combine. Cover the bowl and refrigerate for about 4 hours.

2. Remove rib from marinade and let it sit until it reaches room temperature. Pat dry with paper towels.
3. Preheat your grill to 250°F with lid closed for 15 minutes, using cherry hardwood pellets.
4. Place the ribs on a grill rack. Place the rack on the grill and cook for 2 hours, or until the internal temperature reaches 155°F
5. Meanwhile, combine all the braise ingredients in a disposable aluminum pan.
6. Remove the ribs from the grill and transfer them into the pan containing the sauce. Cover the pan tightly with aluminum foil.
7. Increase the grill heat to 275°F and place the pan on the grill. Cook for 1 hour, or until the internal temperature of the ribs reaches 180°F.
8. Remove the pan from heat and remove the ribs from the pan.
9. Arrange the ribs onto the grill rack and brush all sides of the ribs generously with BBQ sauce.
10. Grill for an additional 20 minutes, turning halfway through.
11. Remove the ribs from heat and let them sit for a few minutes.

12. Serve and enjoy.

Nutrition Facts
Servings: 8

Amount per serving
Calories 409

	% Daily Value*
Total Fat 8.3g	11%
Saturated Fat 2.8g	14%
Cholesterol 166mg	55%
Sodium 1065mg	46%
Total Carbohydrate 19.7g	7%
Dietary Fiber 0.8g	3%
Total Sugars 14.6g	
Protein 59.6g	
Vitamin D 0mcg	0%
Calcium 36mg	3%
Iron 3mg	19%
Potassium 1115mg	24%

Pork Chops

PREP TIME: 10 minutes
COOK TIME: 1 hour 5 minutes
SERVINGS: 4
Ingredients:
- 4 center cut boneless pork chops
- 2 tbsp olive oil

Rub:
- 1 tsp kosher salt or to taste
- 1 tsp Italian seasoning
- 1 tsp Greek seasoning
- ½ tsp cayenne pepper
- 2 tsp brown sugar
- 1 tsp finely chopped fresh rosemary
- 1 tsp ground black pepper

- 1 tsp dried basil
- ½ tsp peppermint
- ½ tsp oregano
- ½ tsp ground cumin

Directions:
1. Start your grill on smoke mode, leaving the lid opened until fire starts.
2. Close the grill lid and preheat grill to 180°F, using hickory hardwood pellet.
3. Combine all the ingredients for the rub ingredients in a small mixing bowl.
4. Drizzle all sides of the pork chops with oil. Liberally season all sides of each pork chop with the rub.
5. Place the pork chops on the grill and smoke, with lid closed, for 45 minutes.
6. Remove the pork chops from the grill and preheat the grill to 450°F.
7. Return the pork chops to the grill and smoke for 20 minutes, or until the internal temperature of the pork chops reaches 150°F.
8. Remove the pork chop from the grill and let it rest for about 15 minutes.
9. Slice and serve.

Nutrition Facts

Servings: 4

Amount per serving

Calories 216

% Daily Value*

Total Fat 11.6g	**15%**
Saturated Fat 2.6g	**13%**
Cholesterol 76mg	**25%**
Sodium 677mg	**29%**
Total Carbohydrate 2.9g	**1%**
Dietary Fiber 0.5g	**2%**
Total Sugars 1.6g	
Protein 25.2g	
Vitamin D 0mcg	0%
Calcium 14mg	1%
Iron 1mg	7%
Potassium 31mg	1%

Smoked Pulled Pork

PREP TIME: 15 minutes
COOK TIME: 8 hours
SERVINGS: 8
Ingredients:
- 1 (6 pounds) pork shoulder (trimmed of excess fat)
- 2 tbsp kosher salt

- 2 tbsp garlic powder
- 1 tbsp ground black pepper
- 1 tbsp cayenne pepper
- 1 tsp paprika
- 1 tsp oregano
- 1 onion (chopped)
- 2 cups apple juice

Directions:
14. To make rub, combine the cayenne, black pepper, garlic, paprika and salt in a small mixing bowl.
15. Rub the pork with the rub mixture generously. The pork butt should be coated with rub.
16. Preheat the grill to 225°F with lid closed for 15 minutes. Use a fruit wood pellet.
17. Place the pork directly on the grill, fat side up. Smoke for 5 hours or until the internal temperature of the pork reaches 160°F.
18. Remove the sirloin from heat adjust the grill temperature to 250°F.
19. Combine the chopped onion and apple juice in a large disposable aluminum foil. Add the roast.

20. Place the pan on the grill and cook for about 3 hour or until the internal temperature of the pork reaches 204°F.
21. Tear off a large portion of aluminum foil and use it to cover the pan tightly. Cook for an additional 3 hour or until the internal temperature of the meat reaches 200°F.
22. Remove the pan from the heat and leave the pork to cool for a few minutes.
23. Drain the braising liquid from the pan, reserving 1 ½ cups of the liquid.
24. Run the reserved braising liquid through a fat separator to remove excess fat.
25. Shred the pork using two forks. Pour in the reserved braising liquid into the pan.
26. Serve and enjoy.

Nutrition Facts

Servings: 8

Amount per serving

Calories 828

	% Daily Value*
Total Fat 46.4g	59%
Saturated Fat 16.4g	82%
Cholesterol 306mg	102%
Sodium 2003mg	87%

Nutrition Facts
Servings: 8

Total Carbohydrate 11g	**4%**
Dietary Fiber 1.2g	**4%**
Total Sugars 7.2g	
Protein 86.9g	
Vitamin D 0mcg	0%
Calcium 80mg	6%
Iron 6mg	32%
Potassium 1316mg	28%

Porchetta

PREP TIME: 30 minutes
COOK TIME: 3 hours
SERVINGS: 12
Ingredients:
- 6 pounds skin on pork belly
- 4 pounds center cut pork loin
- 4 tbsp olive oil
- 1 cup apple juice
- 2 garlic cloves (minced)
- 1 onion (diced)
- 1 ¼ cups grated pecorino Romano cheese

- 1 tsp ground black pepper
- 2 tsp kosher salt
- 3 tbsp fennel seeds
- 1 tbsp freshly chopped rosemary
- 1 tbsp freshly chopped sage
- 1 tbsp freshly chopped thyme
- 1 tbsp grated lemon zest

Rub:
- 1 tbsp chili powder
- 2 tsp grilling seasoning
- 1 tsp salt or to taste
- ½ tsp cayenne
- 1 tsp oregano
- 1 tsp paprika
- 1 tsp mustard powder

Directions:
1. Butterfly the pork loin and place it in the middle of two plastic wraps. On a flat surface, pound the pork evenly until it is ½ inch thick.
2. Combine all the rub ingredients in a small mixing bowl.
3. Place the butterflied pork on a flat surface, cut side up. Season the cut side generously with 1/3 of the rub.

4. Heat up 1 tbsp olive oil in a frying pan over medium to high heat. Add the onion, garlic and fennel seed. Saute until the veggies are tender.
5. Stir the black pepper, 1 tsp kosher salt, rosemary, sage, thyme and lemon zest. Cook for 1 minutes and stir in the cheese.
6. Put the sautéed ingredients on the flat pork and spread evenly. Roll up the pork like you are rolling a burrito. Brush the rolled pork loin with 1 tbsp oil and season with the remaining rub. The loin with butcher's string at 1-inch interval.
7. Roll the pork belly around the pork, skin side out. Brush the pork belly with the remaining oil and season with 1 tsp salt.
8. Set a rack into a roasting pan and place the Porchetta on the rack. Pour the wine into the bottom of the roasting pan.
9. Start your grill on smoke mode, leaving the lid opened for 5 minutes, until fire starts.
10. Close the lid and preheat grill to 325°F, using maple or apple hardwood pellets.
11. Place the roasting pan on the grill and roast Porchetta for about 3 hours or until the internal temperature of the Porchetta reaches 155°F.

12. Remove the Porchetta from heat and let it rest for a few minutes to cool.
13. Remove the butchers string. Slice Porchetta into sizes and serve.

Nutrition Facts

Servings: 12

Amount per serving

Calories 611

% Daily Value*

Total Fat 22.7g	29%
Saturated Fat 7.8g	39%
Cholesterol 252mg	84%
Sodium 1272mg	55%
Total Carbohydrate 6.6g	2%
Dietary Fiber 1.6g	6%
Total Sugars 3.5g	
Protein 89.4g	
Vitamin D 0mcg	0%
Calcium 158mg	12%
Iron 5mg	26%
Potassium 1053mg	22%

Pork Jerky

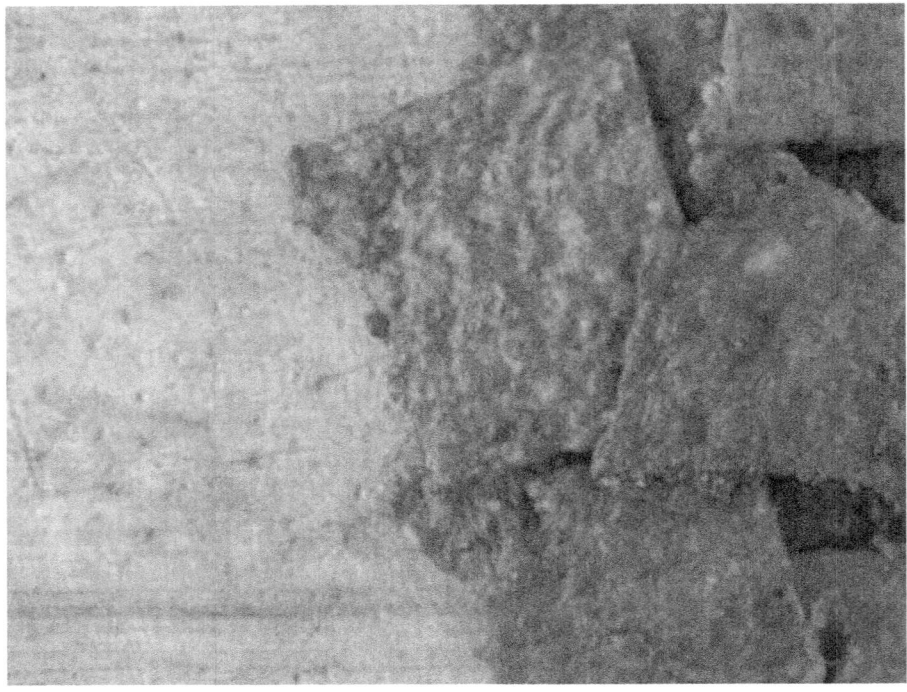

PREP TIME: 15 minutes
COOK TIME: 2 hours 30 minutes
SERVINGS: 12
Ingredients:
- 4 pounds boneless center cut pork (trimmed of excess fat and sliced into ¼ inch thick slices)

Marinade:
- 1/3 cup soy sauce
- 1 cup pineapple juice
- 1 tbsp rice wine vinegar

- 2 tsp black pepper
- 1 tsp red pepper flakes
- 5 tbsp brown sugar
- 1 tsp paprika
- 1 tsp onion powder
- 1 tsp garlic powder
- 2 tsp salt or to taste

Directions:
19. Combine all the marinade ingredients in a mixing bowl and mix until the ingredients are well combined.
20. Put the sliced pork in a gallon sized zip-lock bag and pour the marinade into the bag. Massage the marinade into the pork. Seal the bag and refrigerate for 8 hours.
21. Remove the zip-lock bag from the refrigerator.
22. Activate the pellet grill smoker setting and leave lip opened for 5 minutes until fire starts.
23. Close the lid and preheat your pellet grill to 180°F, using hickory pellet.
24. Remove the pork slices from the marinade and pat them dry with a paper towel.
25. Arrange the pork slices on the grill in a single layer. Smoke the pork for about 2 ½

hours, turning often after the first 1 hour of smoking. The jerky should be dark and dry when it is done.
26. Remove the jerky from the grill and let it sit for about 1 hour to cool.
27. Serve immediately or store in airtight containers and refrigerate for future use.

Nutrition Facts
Servings: 12

Amount per serving

Calories 260

% Daily Value*

Total Fat 11.4g	15%
Saturated Fat 3.8g	19%
Cholesterol 80mg	27%
Sodium 1460mg	63%
Total Carbohydrate 8.6g	3%
Dietary Fiber 0.3g	1%
Total Sugars 7g	
Protein 28.1g	
Vitamin D 0mcg	0%
Calcium 48mg	4%
Iron 1mg	8%

Nutrition Facts
Servings: 12

Potassium 64mg 1%

Chapter Four

Seafood Recipes

Grilled Lobster Tail

PREP TIME: 10 minutes
COOK TIME: 15 minutes
SERVINGS: 4
Ingredients:
- 2 (8 ounces each) lobster tails

- 1/4 tsp old bay seasoning
- ½ tsp oregano
- 1 tsp paprika
- Juice from one lemon
- 1/4 tsp Himalayan salt
- 1/4 tsp freshly ground black pepper
- 1/4 tsp onion powder
- 2 tbsp freshly chopped parsley
- ¼ cup melted butter

Directions:
1. Slice the tail in the middle with a kitchen shear. Pull the shell apart slightly and run your hand through the meat to separate the meat partially, keeping it attached to the base of the tail partially.
2. Combine the old bay seasoning, paprika, oregano, salt, pepper and onion powder in a mixing bowl.
3. Drizzle lobster tail with lemon juice and season generously with the seasoning mixture.
4. Preheat your wood pellet smoker to 450°F, using apple wood pellets.
5. Place the lobster tail directly on the grill grate, meat side down. Cook for about 15

minutes or until the internal temperature of the tails reaches 140°F.
6. Remove the tails from the grill and let them rest for a few minutes to cool.
7. Drizzle melted butter over the tails.
8. Serve and garnish with fresh chopped parsley.

Nutrition Facts

Servings: 4

Amount per serving
Calories 146

	% Daily Value*
Total Fat 11.7g	15%
Saturated Fat 7.3g	37%
Cholesterol 56mg	19%
Sodium 295mg	13%
Total Carbohydrate 2.1g	1%
Dietary Fiber 0.8g	3%
Total Sugars 0.5g	
Protein 9.3g	
Vitamin D 8mcg	40%
Calcium 15mg	1%
Iron 0mg	3%

Nutrition Facts
Servings: 4

Potassium 53mg   1%

Halibut

PREP TIME: 10 minutes
COOK TIME: 30 minutes
SERVINGS: 4
Ingredients:
- 1 pound fresh halibut filet (cut into 4 equal sizes)
- 1 tbsp fresh lemon juice
- 2 garlic cloves (minced)
- 2 tsp soy sauce

- ½ tsp ground black pepper
- ½ tsp onion powder
- 2 tbsp honey
- ½ tsp oregano
- 1 tsp dried basil
- 2 tbsp butter (melted)
- Maple syrup for serving

Directions:
1. In a mixing bowl, combine the lemon juice, honey, soy sauce, onion powder, oregano, dried basil, pepper and garlic.
2. Brush the halibut filets generously with the filet the mixture. Wrap the filets with aluminum foil and refrigerate for 4 hours.
3. Remove the filets from the refrigerator and let them sit for about 2 hours, or until they are at room temperature.
4. Activate your wood pellet grill on smoke, leaving the lid opened for 5 minutes or until fire starts.
5. Close the lid and preheat your grill to 275°F 15 minutes, using fruit wood pellets.
6. Place the halibut filets directly on the grill grate and smoke for 30 minutes or until the internal temperature of the fish reaches 135°F.

7. Remove the filets from the grill and let them rest for 10 minutes.
8. Serve and top with maple syrup to taste

Nutrition Facts

Servings: 4

Amount per serving

Calories 180

	% Daily Value*
Total Fat 6.3g	8%
Saturated Fat 3.7g	18%
Cholesterol 35mg	12%
Sodium 247mg	11%
Total Carbohydrate 10g	4%
Dietary Fiber 0.3g	1%
Total Sugars 8.9g	
Protein 20.6g	
Vitamin D 4mcg	20%
Calcium 11mg	1%
Iron 0mg	2%
Potassium 34mg	1%

Grilled Salmon

PREP TIME: 10 minutes
COOK TIME: 30 minutes
SERVINGS: 6
Ingredients:
- 2 pounds salmon (cut into fillets)
- 1/2 cup low sodium soy sauce
- 2 garlic cloves (grated)
- 4 tbsp olive oil
- 2 tbsp honey
- 1 tsp ground black pepper

- ½ tsp smoked paprika
- ½ tsp Italian seasoning
  Garnish:
- 2 tbsp chopped green onion

Directions:
1. In a large mixing bowl, combine the honey, pepper, paprika, Italian seasoning, garlic, soy sauce and olive oil. Add the salmon fillets and toss to combine. Cover the bowl and refrigerate for 1 hour.
2. Remove the fillets from the marinade and let it sit for about 2 hours, or until it is at room temperature.
3. Start the wood pellet on smoke, leaving the lid opened for 5 minutes, or until fire starts.
4. Close the lid and preheat grill to 350°F for 15 minutes.
5. Grease the grill grate with oil and arrange the fillets on the grill grate, skin side up. Close the grill lid and cook for 4 minutes.
6. Flip the fillets and cook for additional 25 minutes or until the fish is flaky.
7. Remove the fillets from heat and let it sit for a few minutes.
8. Serve warm and garnish with chopped green onion.

Nutrition Facts

Servings: 6

Amount per serving

Calories 317

	% Daily Value*
Total Fat 18.8g	24%
Saturated Fat 2.7g	13%
Cholesterol 67mg	22%
Sodium 776mg	34%
Total Carbohydrate 8.3g	3%
Dietary Fiber 0.4g	1%
Total Sugars 6.2g	
Protein 30.6g	
Vitamin D 0mcg	0%
Calcium 61mg	5%
Iron 2mg	9%
Potassium 635mg	14%

BBQ Shrimp

PREP TIME: 20 minutes
COOK TIME: 8 minutes
SERVINGS: 6
Ingredients:
- 2 pound raw shrimp (peeled and deveined)
- ¼ cup extra virgin olive oil
- ½ tsp paprika
- ½ tsp red pepper flakes
- 2 garlic cloves (minced)
- 1 tsp cumin
- 1 lemon (juiced)
- 1 tsp kosher salt

- 1 tbsp chili paste
- Bamboo or wooden skewers (soaked for 30 minutes, at least)

Directions:
1. In a large mixing bowl, combine the pepper flakes, cumin, lemon, salt, chili, paprika, garlic and olive oil. Add the shrimp and toss to combine.
2. Transfer the shrimp and marinade into a zip-lock bag and refrigerate for 4 hours.
3. Remove the shrimp from the marinade and let it rest until it is a room temperature.
4. Start your grill on smoke, leaving the lid opened for 5 minutes, or until fire starts. Use hickory wood pellet.
5. Close the lid and preheat the grill to HIGH for 15 minutes.
6. Thread shrimps onto skewers and arrange the skewers on the grill grate.
7. Smoke shrimps for 8 minutes, 4 minutes per side.
8. Serve and enjoy.

Nutrition Facts
Servings: 6

Amount per serving

Nutrition Facts

Servings: 6

Calories 267

% Daily Value*

Total Fat 11.6g	**15%**
Saturated Fat 2g	**10%**
Cholesterol 319mg	**106%**
Sodium 788mg	**34%**
Total Carbohydrate 4.9g	**2%**
Dietary Fiber 0.4g	**2%**
Total Sugars 1g	
Protein 34.9g	
Vitamin D 0mcg	0%
Calcium 149mg	11%
Iron 1mg	5%
Potassium 287mg	6%

Grilled Tuna

PREP TIME: 5 minutes
COOK TIME: 4 minutes
SERVINGS: 4
Ingredients:
- 4 (6 ounce each) tuna steaks (1 inch thick)
- 1 lemon (juiced)
- 1 clove garlic (minced)
- 1 tsp chili
- 2 tbsp extra virgin olive oil
- 1 cup white wine
- 3 tbsp brown sugar
- 1 tsp rosemary

Directions:
1. In a large mixing bowl, combine the chili, lemon, white wine, sugar, rosemary, olive oil and garlic. Add the tuna steaks and toss to combine.
2. Transfer the tuna and marinade to a zip-lock bag. Refrigerate for 3 hours.
3. Remove the tuna steaks from the marinade and let them rest for about 1 hour, or until the steaks are at room temperature.
4. Start your grill on smoke, leaving the lid opened for 5 minutes, or until fire starts. Use hickory or mesquite wood pellet.
5. Close the grill lid and preheat the grill on HIGH for 15 minutes.
6. Grease the grill grate with oil and place the tuna on the grill grate. Grill tuna steaks for 4 minutes, 2 minutes per side.
7. Remove the tuna from the grill and let them rest for a few minutes.
8. Serve and enjoy.

Nutrition Facts
Servings: 4

Amount per serving
Calories 455

% Daily Value*

Nutrition Facts

Servings: 4

Total Fat 17.8g	**23%**
Saturated Fat 3.8g	**19%**
Cholesterol 84mg	**28%**
Sodium 97mg	**4%**
Total Carbohydrate 10.2g	**4%**
Dietary Fiber 0.6g	**2%**
Total Sugars 7.4g	
Protein 51.2g	
Vitamin D 0mcg	0%
Calcium 37mg	3%
Iron 3mg	15%
Potassium 648mg	14%

Oyster in Shell

PREP TIME: 25 minutes
COOK TIME: 8 minutes
SERVINGS: 4
Ingredients:

- 12 medium oysters * note that all oysters should be completely closed. Opened/dead oysters are of no use here.
- 1 tsp oregano
- 1 lemon (juiced)
- 1 tsp freshly ground black pepper
- 6 tbsp unsalted butter (melted)
- 1 tsp salt or more to taste

- 2 garlic cloves (minced)

Garnish:
- 2 ½ tbsp grated parmesan cheese
- 2 tbsp freshly chopped parsley

Directions:
1. Start by scrubbing the outside of the shell with a scrub brush under cold running water to remove dirt.
2. Hold an oyster in a towel, flat side up. Insert an oyster knife in the hinge of the oyster. Twist the knife with pressure to pop open the oyster. Run the knife along the oyster hinge to open the shell completely. Discard the top shell.
3. Gently run the knife under the oyster to loosen the oyster foot from the bottom shell.
4. Repeat step 2 and 3 for the remaining oysters.
5. Combine melted butter, lemon, pepper, salt, garlic and oregano in a mixing bowl.
6. Pour ½ to 1 tsp of the butter mixture on each oyster.
7. Start your wood pellet grill on smoke, leaving the lid opened for 5 minutes, or until fire starts.

8. Close the lid and preheat the grill to HIGH with lid closed for 15 minutes.
9. Gently arrange the oysters onto the grill grate.
10. Grill oyster for 6 to 8 minutes or until the oyster juice is bubbling and the oyster is plump.
11. Remove oysters from heat. Serve and top with grated parmesan and chopped parsley.

Nutrition Facts

Servings: 4

Amount per serving

Calories 200

% Daily Value*

Total Fat 19.2g	25%
Saturated Fat 11.9g	59%
Cholesterol 66mg	22%
Sodium 788mg	34%
Total Carbohydrate 3.9g	1%
Dietary Fiber 0.8g	3%
Total Sugars 0.7g	
Protein 4.6g	
Vitamin D 12mcg	62%

Nutrition Facts
Servings: 4

Calcium 93mg	7%
Iron 2mg	14%
Potassium 120mg	3%

Grilled King Crab Legs

PREP TIME: 10 minutes
COOK TIME: 25 minutes
SERVINGS: 4

Ingredients:
- 4 pounds king crab legs (split)
- 4 tbsp lemon juice
- 2 tbsp garlic powder
- 1 cup butter (melted)
- 2 tsp brown sugar
- 2 tsp paprika
- 2 tsp ground black pepper or more to taste

Directions:
1. In a mixing bowl, combine the lemon juice, butter, sugar, garlic, paprika and pepper.
2. Arrange the split crab on a baking sheet, split side up.
3. Drizzle ¾ of the butter mixture over the crab legs.
4. Configure your pellet grill for indirect cooking and preheat it to 225°F, using mesquite wood pellets.
5. Arrange the crab legs onto the grill grate, shell side down.
6. Cover the grill and cook 25 minutes.
7. Remove the crab legs from the grill.
8. Serve and top with the remaining butter mixture.

Nutrition Facts

Servings: 4

Amount per serving

Calories 894

	% Daily Value*
Total Fat 53.2g	68%
Saturated Fat 29.3g	147%
Cholesterol 374mg	125%
Sodium 5189mg	226%
Total Carbohydrate 6.1g	2%
Dietary Fiber 1.2g	4%
Total Sugars 3g	
Protein 88.6g	
Vitamin D 32mcg	159%
Calcium 301mg	23%
Iron 4mg	22%
Potassium 119mg	3%

Cajun Smoked Catfish

PREP TIME: 15 minutes
COOK TIME: 2 hours
SERVINGS: 4
Ingredients:
- 4 catfish fillets (5 ounces each)
- ½ cup Cajun seasoning
- 1 tsp ground black pepper
- 1 tbsp smoked paprika

- 1/4 tsp cayenne pepper
- 1 tsp hot sauce
- 1 tsp granulated garlic
- 1 tsp onion powder
- 1 tsp thyme
- 1 tsp salt or more to taste
- 2 tbsp chopped fresh parsley

Directions:
1. Pour water into the bottom of a square or rectangular dish. Add 4 tbsp salt. Arrange the catfish fillets into the dish. Cover the dish and refrigerate for 3 to 4 hours.
2. Meanwhile, combine the paprika, cayenne, hot sauce, onion, salt, thyme, garlic, pepper and Cajun seasoning in a mixing bowl.
3. Remove the fish from the dish and let it sit for a few minutes, or until it is at room temperature. Pat the fish fillets dry with a paper towel.
4. Rub the seasoning mixture over each fillet generously.
5. Start your grill on smoke, leaving the lid opened for 5 minutes, or until fire starts.
6. Close the lid and preheat the grill to 200°F, using mesquite hardwood pellets.

7. Arrange the fish fillets onto the grill grate and close the grill. Cook for about 2 hours, or until the fish is flaky.
8. Remove the fillets from the grill and let the fillets rest for a few minutes to cool.
9. Serve and garnish with chopped fresh parsley.

Nutrition Facts

Servings: 4

Amount per serving

Calories 204

	% Daily Value*
Total Fat 11.1g	14%
Saturated Fat 2g	10%
Cholesterol 67mg	22%
Sodium 991mg	43%
Total Carbohydrate 2.7g	1%
Dietary Fiber 1.1g	4%
Total Sugars 0.6g	
Protein 22.9g	
Vitamin D 0mcg	0%
Calcium 29mg	2%
Iron 3mg	17%

Nutrition Facts
Servings: 4

Potassium 532mg   11%

Smoked Scallops

PREP TIME: 10 minutes
COOK TIME: 15 minutes
SERVINGS: 6
Ingredients:
- 2 pounds sea scallops
- 4 tbsp salted butter

- 2 tbsp lemon juice
- ½ tsp ground black pepper
- 1 garlic clove (minced)
- 1 kosher tsp salt
- 1 tsp freshly chopped tarragon

Directions:
1. Pat the scallops dry with paper towels and season all sides of the scallops with pepper and salt.
2. Place you're a cast iron pan in your grill and preheat the grill to 400°F with lid closed for 15 minutes.
3. Combine the butter and garlic in hot cast iron pan. Add the scallops and stir. Close grill lid and cook for 8 minutes.
4. Flip the scallops and cook for an additional 7 minutes.
5. Remove the scallop from heat and let it rest for a few minutes.
6. Stir in the chopped tarragon. Serve and top with lemon juice.

Nutrition Facts
Servings: 6

Amount per serving
Calories 204

Nutrition Facts
Servings: 6

	% Daily Value*
Total Fat 8.9g	11%
Saturated Fat 5g	25%
Cholesterol 70mg	23%
Sodium 687mg	30%
Total Carbohydrate 4g	1%
Dietary Fiber 0.1g	0%
Total Sugars 0.1g	
Protein 25.6g	
Vitamin D 5mcg	27%
Calcium 42mg	3%
Iron 1mg	3%
Potassium 503mg	11%

Grilled Tilapia

PREP TIME: 10 minutes
COOK TIME: 20 minutes
SERVINGS: 6
Ingredients:
- 2 tsp dried parsley
- ½ tsp garlic powder
- 1 tsp cayenne pepper
- ½ tsp ground black pepper
- ½ tsp thyme
- ½ tsp dried basil

- ½ tsp oregano
- 3 tbsp olive oil
- ½ tsp lemon pepper
- 1 tsp kosher salt
- 1 lemon (juiced)
- 6 tilapia fillets
- 1 ½ tsp creole seafood seasoning

Directions:
1. In a mixing bowl, combine the garlic powder, cayenne, black pepper, thyme, basil, oregano, lemon pepper, salt and parsley.
2. Brush the fillets with oil and lemon juice.
3. Liberally, season all sides of the tilapia fillets with the seasoning mix.
4. Preheat your grill to 325°F with lid closed for 15 minutes, using mesquite or hickory hardwood pellets.
5. Place a non-stick BBQ grilling try on the grill and arrange the tilapia fillets onto it.
6. Grill for 15 to 20 minutes or until the temperature of the thickest part of the meat reaches 145°F.
7. Remove the fillets from heat and let them sit for a few minutes.
8. Serve and top with

Nutrition Facts

Servings: 6

Amount per serving

Calories　　　　　　　　　176

　　　　　　　　　　　　　　% Daily Value*

Total Fat 9.6g	**12%**
Saturated Fat 2g	**10%**
Cholesterol 50mg	**17%**
Sodium 982mg	**43%**
Total Carbohydrate 1.5g	**1%**
Dietary Fiber 0.5g	**2%**
Total Sugars 0.3g	
Protein 22.3g	
Vitamin D 0mcg	0%
Calcium 28mg	2%
Iron 1mg	6%
Potassium 350mg	7%

Shrimp Scampi

PREP TIME: 5 minutes
COOK TIME: 10 minutes
SERVINGS: 4
Ingredients:

- 1 ¼ pound large shrimp (peeled and deveined)
- 1 medium red bell pepper (finely chopped)
- 1 tsp ground black pepper or to taste
- ¼ tsp crushed red bell pepper flakes
- 1 tsp salt or to taste
- 4 tbsp butter (melted)
- 2 tbsp olive oil

- 2 garlic cloves (grated)
- ¼ cup dry white wine
- 2 tbsp fresh lemon juice
- 3 tbsp chopped fresh parsley

Directions:
1. Place a cast iron skillet in the grill and preheat grill to 400°F.
2. Combine the butter and oil in the skillet.
3. Add the onion, garlic and tomato and stir cook for about 2 minutes.
4. Stir in the white wine, crush red pepper flakes, ground black pepper and salt.
5. Bring to a boil and simmer for about 2 to 3 minutes or until the liquid content has reduces by half.
6. Add the shrimps, close the lid and grill for 10 minutes
7. Stir in the lemon juice and chopped parsley. Remove the skillet from heat.
8. Serve warm over rice or pasta and enjoy.

Nutrition Facts
Servings: 6

Amount per serving
Calories   **176**

Nutrition Facts
Servings: 6

	% Daily Value*
Total Fat 9.6g	12%
Saturated Fat 2g	10%
Cholesterol 50mg	17%
Sodium 982mg	43%
Total Carbohydrate 1.5g	1%
Dietary Fiber 0.5g	2%
Total Sugars 0.3g	
Protein 22.3g	
Vitamin D 0mcg	0%
Calcium 28mg	2%
Iron 1mg	6%
Potassium 350mg	7%

Smoked Shrimp

PREP TIME: 35 minutes
COOK TIME: 10 minutes
SERVINGS: 4
Ingredients:
- 12 large shrimps (peeled and vein removed)
- 2 tbsp butter (softened)
- 1tsp garlic
- 4 tbsp parmesan cheese
- ½ tsp sea salt or to taste
- ½ tsp ground black pepper

- 6 tbsp almond flour or coconut flour
- 2 tbsp olive oil

Garnish:
- Fresh chopped parsley

Directions:
1. Combine the garlic, salt, pepper and olive oil in a large mixing bowl.
2. Add the shrimps and toss until the shrimps are all coated.
3. Cover the mixing bowl and place it in the fridge. Refrigerate for about 30 minutes.
4. Start your grill on smoke mode, leaving the lid opened until fire starts.
5. Close the lid and preheat the grill to 450°F for 15 minutes.
6. Grease a baking sheet with a non-stick cooking spray. Set aside.
7. In another mixing bowl, mix the almond flour and cheese.
8. Add the marinated shrimps to the flour-cheese mixture and toss until the shrimps are all coated.
9. Arrange the shrimps into the baking sheet in a single layer.

10. Place the baking sheet on the grill and smoke until the shrimps are crispy. This will take about 10- 12 minutes.
11. Remove the baking sheet from the grill and leave the shrimps to cool for a few minutes.
12. Serve and garnish with chopped fresh parsley and serve.

Nutrition Facts

Servings: 4

Amount per serving

Calories 222

% Daily Value*

Total Fat 20.3g	26%
Saturated Fat 6.4g	32%
Cholesterol 57mg	19%
Sodium 401mg	17%
Total Carbohydrate 3.2g	1%
Dietary Fiber 1.2g	4%
Total Sugars 0.4g	
Protein 9.1g	
Vitamin D 4mcg	20%
Calcium 124mg	10%
Iron 1mg	3%

Nutrition Facts
Servings: 4

Potassium 36mg　　　1%

Chapter Five

Wild Meat Recipes

Goat Chops

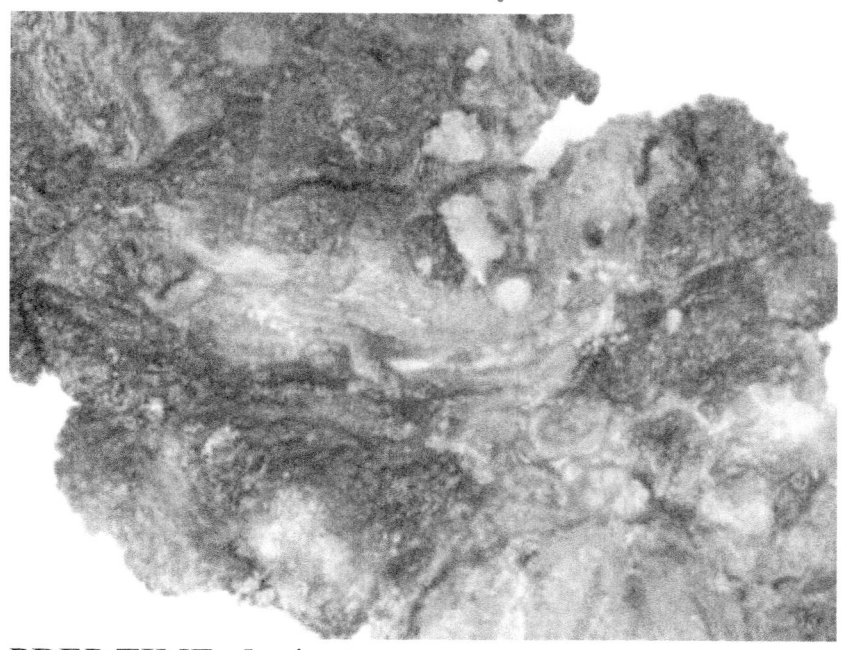

PREP TIME: 5 minutes
COOK TIME: 8 minutes
SERVINGS: 8
Ingredients:
- 8 1-inch thick goat chops

Marinade:

- 6 garlic cloves (minced)
- 1 tbsp dried oregano
- ¼ tsp salt
- 1 tsp ground black pepper
- ½ cup dry white wine
- 1 lemon (juiced)
- 1 tbsp grated lemon zest
- 1 onion (chopped)

Directions:
1. Combine all the marinade ingredients in a mixing bowl. Add the goat chops and toss to combine. Leave the goat chops in the marinade for about 30 minutes.
2. Start the grill on smoke mode, leaving the lid opened for 5 minutes for fire to start.
3. Close the lid and preheat the grill to HIGH, with lid closed for 15 minutes.
4. Place the goat chops on the grill grate and smoke for 8 minutes, 4 minutes per side.
5. Remove goat chops from heat and let it cool for a few minutes.
6. Serve.

Nutrition Facts
Servings: 8

Amount per serving

Nutrition Facts
Servings: 8

Calories 147

% Daily Value*

Total Fat 2.7g	**3%**
Saturated Fat 0.8g	**4%**
Cholesterol 64mg	**21%**
Sodium 149mg	**6%**
Total Carbohydrate 3.6g	**1%**
Dietary Fiber 0.9g	**3%**
Total Sugars 0.9g	
Protein 23.5g	
Vitamin D 0mcg	0%
Calcium 35mg	3%
Iron 4mg	20%
Potassium 411mg	9%

Smoked Goose Breast

PREP TIME: 15 minutes
COOK TIME: 45 minutes
SERVINGS: 8
Ingredients:
- 8 goose breasts

Marinade:
- 4 tbsp soy sauce
- 5 tbsp brown sugar
- 4 tbsp honey
- 1 tsp garlic powder

- 1 tbsp Dijon mustard
- 1/3 cup olive oil
- ½ cup pineapple juice
- 1 tsp paprika
- ½ tsp cayenne pepper

Directions:
1. In a large mixing bowl, combine the soy sauce, mustard, paprika, cayenne pepper, pineapple juice, olive oil, garlic, honey and brown sugar.
2. Add the goose breast and massage the marinade into the breast. Cover the bowl and refrigerate for 3 hours.
3. Remove the goose breasts from the marinade and let the breasts rest until they are at room temperature. Pat dry with paper towels. Reserve 1 cup of the marinade.
4. Start your grill on smoke mode, leaving the lid opened for 5 minutes for fire to start.
5. Close the lid and preheat the grill to 300°F using hickory hardwood pellets.
6. Arrange the goose breast on the grill grate and smoke for 30 minutes.
7. Brush the reserved marinade over the goose breast. Smoke for additional about

15 minutes, or until the internal temperature of the goose breast reaches 165°F.

Nutrition Facts

Servings: 8

Amount per serving
Calories 262

	% Daily Value*
Total Fat 12.6g	16%
Saturated Fat 1.2g	6%
Cholesterol 142mg	47%
Sodium 476mg	21%
Total Carbohydrate 17.3g	6%
Dietary Fiber 0.3g	1%
Total Sugars 15.9g	
Protein 23.8g	
Vitamin D 0mcg	0%
Calcium 11mg	1%
Iron 0mg	2%
Potassium 65mg	1%

Smoked Venison Tenderloin

PREP TIME: 15 minutes
COOK TIME: 2 hours
SERVINGS: 4
Ingredients:
- 1-pound venison tenderloin or backstrap
- 1 tbsp ground black pepper
- 2/3 cup olive oil
- 5 garlic cloves (minced)
- 1 tsp dried thyme
- 1 tsp dried oregano

- 1 tsp paprika
- 1 tsp freshly chopped peppermint
- 1 tbsp kosher salt
- 1 cup balsamic vinegar

Directions:
1. In a large mixing bowl, combine the pepper, oil, garlic, thyme, oregano, paprika, peppermint, salt and vinegar.
2. Pour the mixture into a zip-lock bag and add the tenderloin. Seal the bag and refrigerate for 10 hours or overnight.
3. Remove the tenderloin from the marinade and let it sit for about 1 hour, until it comes to room temperature.
4. Start your grill on smoke mode and leave the lid opened for 5 minutes, until the fire starts.
5. Close the grill and preheat the grill to 225°F, using apple hardwood pellets
6. Place the tenderloin on the grill and smoke for 1 ½ - 2 hours, or until the internal temperature of the meat reaches 140°F.
7. Remove the tenderloin from heat and let it sit for a few minutes.
8. Cut into sizes and serve.

Nutrition Facts
Servings: 4

Amount per serving
Calories 483

	% Daily Value*
Total Fat 36.5g	**47%**
Saturated Fat 6.2g	**31%**
Cholesterol 100mg	**33%**
Sodium 1814mg	**79%**
Total Carbohydrate 3.6g	**1%**
Dietary Fiber 1g	**4%**
Total Sugars 0.4g	
Protein 34.5g	
Vitamin D 0mcg	0%
Calcium 37mg	3%
Iron 6mg	34%
Potassium 595mg	13%

Smoked Rabbit

PREP TIME: 15 minutes
COOK TIME: 3 hours
SERVINGS: 4
Ingredients:
- 1 (3 pounds) whole rabbit
- 1 tbsp dried rosemary
- 1/3 cup olive oil
- 1 tbsp dried thyme
- 1 tbsp cracked black pepper
- 1 tsp sea salt
- ½ cup dry white wine

- 1 cup apple juice
- 1 tbsp dried oregano
- 1 tbsp freshly grated lemon zest

Directions:
1. In a large baking dish, combine the rosemary, oil, thyme, salt, wine, apple juice, oregano, lemon and pepper.
2. Place the whole rabbit inside the dish and massage the marinade into the rabbit. Cover the baking dish tightly with aluminum foil. Refrigerate for 8 hours or overnight.
3. Remove the rabbit from the marinade and let it rest until it comes to room temperature. Pat dry with paper towels.
4. Place a rack on a roasting pan and pour water into the bottom of the pan. Place the rabbit on the rack.
5. Preheat your pellet grill to 240°F with lid closed for 15 minutes.
6. Place the roasting pan on the grill and cook rabbit for 3 hours or until the internal temperature of the rabbit reaches 165°F. Flip halfway through.
7. Remove the rabbit from the grill and let it sit for a few minutes to cool.
8. Cut rabbit into sizes and serve.

Nutrition Facts

Servings: 4

Amount per serving

Calories 676

% Daily Value*

Total Fat 48.5g	62%
Saturated Fat 14.2g	71%
Cholesterol 258mg	86%
Sodium 689mg	30%
Total Carbohydrate 12.5g	5%
Dietary Fiber 1.7g	6%
Total Sugars 8.1g	
Protein 70.3g	
Vitamin D 0mcg	0%
Calcium 165mg	13%
Iron 2mg	12%
Potassium 1305mg	28%

Spatchcock Smoked Quail

PREP TIME: 15 minutes
COOK TIME: 1 hour
SERVINGS: 4
Ingredients:
- 4 quails
- 2 tbsp finely chopped fresh parsley
- 1 tbsp finely chopped fresh rosemary
- 2 tbsp finely chopped fresh thyme
- ½ cup melted butter
- 1 tsp garlic powder
- 1 tsp onion powder
- 1 tsp ground black pepper
- 2 tsp salt or to taste

- 2 tbsp finely chopped scallions

Directions:
10. Remove the giblets from the quails and rinse quails, in and out, under cold running water.
11. Place one quail on a working surface, breast side down. Use a poultry shear to cut the quail along both sides of the backbone to remove the turkey back bone.
12. Flip the quail over, back side down. Now, press the turkey down to flatten it.
13. Repeat step 2 and 3 for the remaining quails.
14. In a mixing bowl, combine the parsley, rosemary, scallions, thyme, butter, pepper, salt, garlic and onion powder.
15. Rub butter mixture over all sides of the quails.
16. Configure your grill for smoking. Preheat your grill to 375°F with lid closed for 15 minutes.
17. Place the quails directly on the grill grate and cook for 30 minutes and smoke quails for 1 hour or until the internal temperature of the quails reaches 165°F.
18. Remove the turkey from the grill and let it rest for a few minutes.

19. Cut into sizes and serve.

Nutrition Facts

Servings: 4

Amount per serving
Calories 279

% Daily Value*

Total Fat 27.2g	**35%**
Saturated Fat 15.8g	**79%**
Cholesterol 85mg	**28%**
Sodium 1346mg	**59%**
Total Carbohydrate 3.1g	**1%**
Dietary Fiber 1.2g	**4%**
Total Sugars 0.5g	
Protein 7.2g	
Vitamin D 16mcg	79%
Calcium 59mg	5%
Iron 4mg	20%
Potassium 65mg	1%

Smoked Pheasant

PREP TIME: 15 minutes
COOK TIME: 5 hours
SERVINGS: 5
Ingredients:
- 2 whole pheasants
- 4 tbsp brown sugar
- 1 tbsp kosher salt
- 1 tbsp black peppercorns
- 4 cups water
- 2 cups maple syrup
- 1 cup pineapple juice

- 1 tbsp Dijon mustard

Directions:
1. To brine the pheasants, combine the water, salt, peppercorns and brown sugar in a large baking dish. Add the pheasant. Pour in more water, if needed, until the pheasants are completely submerged.
2. Remove the pheasants from the brine and let them sit for about 1 hour, until they are at room temperature. Pat dry with paper towels
3. Start your grill on smoke mode and leave the lip opened until fire starts.
4. Close the lid and preheat grill to 200°F, using hickory hardwood pellets.
5. Place the pheasants on the grill and smoke for 1 hour.
6. Meanwhile, combine the maple syrup, apple juice and mustard in a saucepan over medium to high heat.
7. Bring to a boil, reduce the heat and simmer until sauce thickens and reduces by half.
8. Baste the pheasants with the sauce. Continue cooking, basting pheasants with sauce at 30 minutes interval, until the internal temperature of the pheasants reaches 165°F.

9. Remove the pheasants from heat and let them to cool for a few minutes.
10. Cut pheasant to sizes and serve.

Nutrition Facts

Servings: 5

Amount per serving

Calories 434

% Daily Value*

Total Fat 3g	4%
Saturated Fat 0.9g	5%
Cholesterol 0mg	0%
Sodium 1451mg	63%
Total Carbohydrate 99g	36%
Dietary Fiber 0.5g	2%
Total Sugars 87g	
Protein 6.3g	
Vitamin D 0mcg	0%
Calcium 111mg	9%
Iron 2mg	12%
Potassium 354mg	8%

Rabbit Stew

PREP TIME: 15 minutes
COOK TIME: 2 hours
SERVINGS: 4
Ingredients:
- 1 (3 pounds) rabbit (cut into bite sizes)
- ¼ cup olive oil
- 1 medium onion (chopped)
- 1 carrot (diced)
- 1 stalk celery (diced)
- 2 roma tomato (sliced)
- 1 red bell pepper (sliced)

- 2 garlic cloves (minced)
- 1 cup red wine
- 4 cups chicken broth
- 2 bay leaves
- 2 tbsp flour
- 1 tsp dried thyme
- 1 tsp salt
- 1 tsp ground black pepper

Directions:
1. Heat up the olive oil in a large Dutch grill over medium to high heat.
2. Add the rabbit pieces and sear until all sides of the rabbit pieces are browned.
3. Use a slotted spoon to transfer the rabbit pieces to a paper towel lined plate to drain.
4. Add the onion and garlic. Saute until the veggies are tender.
5. Add the tomatoes, carrot and red bell pepper. Saute for 3 minutes, stirring often. Stir in the flour and cook for 1 minute.
6. Pour in the chicken broth and red wine. Stir in the salt.
7. Add the browned rabbit pieces and the bay leaves.
8. Bring mixture to a boil, reduce the heat and simmer for a few minutes.

9. Start your pellet grill on smoke mode. Leave the lid opened for 5 minutes, until fire starts.
10. Close the lid and preheat the grill to 300°F, using cherry or apple hardwood pellets.
11. Place the Dutch grill on the grill and cook for about 2 hours, or until the rabbit pieces are tender.

Nutrition Facts

Servings: 4

Amount per serving

Calories 932

	% Daily Value*
Total Fat 41.9g	**54%**
Saturated Fat 10.4g	**52%**
Cholesterol 279mg	**93%**
Sodium 1531mg	**67%**
Total Carbohydrate 17.7g	**6%**
Dietary Fiber 2.9g	**10%**
Total Sugars 7.2g	
Protein 106.1g	
Vitamin D 0mcg	0%
Calcium 108mg	8%

Nutrition Facts
Servings: 4

Iron 11mg	64%
Potassium 1949mg	41%

Grilled Antelope

PREP TIME: 10 minutes
COOK TIME: 15 minutes
SERVINGS: 8
Ingredients:

- 1 pound antelope steak (slices into 1 inch thick slices)

Marinade:
- 4 tbsp olive oil
- ½ tsp dried rosemary
- 2 garlic cloves (minced)
- 1 lemon (juice)
- ¼ cup balsamic vinegar
- ½ tsp salt or to taste
- 1 tsp onion powder
- ¼ tsp thyme
- 1 tsp oregano
- 1 tsp paprika

Directions:
1. Combine all the marinade ingredients in a large mixing bowl. Add the steaks and toss to combine. Cover the bowl and marinate for 8 hours or overnight.
2. Remove the steaks from the marinade and let the steak rest, until they are at room temperature. Pat dry with paper towels.
3. Start your grill on smoke mode and leave the lid opened until fire starts.
4. Close the lid and preheat the grill to HIGH.
5. Arrange the steaks onto a smoking rack in a single layer.

6. Place the rack on the grill and smoke steaks for 15 minutes, turning halfway through.
7. Remove the steaks from heat and let the steak rest for a few minutes.
8. Serve and enjoy.

Nutrition Facts

Servings: 8

Amount per serving

Calories 159

% Daily Value*

Total Fat 8.6g	11%
Saturated Fat 1.6g	8%
Cholesterol 71mg	24%
Sodium 180mg	8%
Total Carbohydrate 1.9g	1%
Dietary Fiber 0.5g	2%
Total Sugars 0.5g	
Protein 16.9g	
Vitamin D 0mcg	0%
Calcium 14mg	1%
Iron 3mg	15%
Potassium 264mg	6%

Elk Kebabs

PREP TIME: 10 minutes
COOK TIME: 12 minutes
SERVINGS: 4
Ingredients:
- 2 elk steaks (cut into 2-inch cubes)
- 1 large bell pepper (sliced)
- 1 large yellow bell pepper (sliced)
- 1 large green bell pepper (sliced)
- 1 onion (sliced)

- 10 medium cremini mushrooms (destemmed and halved)
- Wooden or bamboo skewers (soaked in water for 30 minutes, at least)

Marinade:
- 1 tbsp soy sauce
- 1 tsp garlic powder
- ½ tsp ground black pepper
- 1 tbsp Worcestershire sauce
- 1 tbsp lemon juice
- 1 tsp onion powder
- 3 tbsp olive oil
- 1 tsp paprika

Directions:
15. In a large mixing bowl, combine all the marinade ingredients. Add the elk and mushroom. Toss to combine. Cover the bowl tightly with aluminum foil and refrigerate for 8 hours.
16. Remove the mushroom and elk from the marinade.
17. Thread the bell peppers, onion, mushroom and elk onto skewers to make kabobs.
18. Preheat your grill to HIGH with lid closed for 15 minutes, using mesquite hardwood pellets.

19. Arrange the kebobs onto the grill grate and grill for 12 minutes, 6 minutes per side, or until the internal temperature of the elk reaches 145°F.
20. Remove kebabs from heat.
21. Serve warm and enjoy.

Nutrition Facts

Servings: 4

Amount per serving

Calories 292

% Daily Value*

Total Fat 13.8g	**18%**
Saturated Fat 2.6g	**13%**
Cholesterol 64mg	**21%**
Sodium 330mg	**14%**
Total Carbohydrate 12.4g	**4%**
Dietary Fiber 2.7g	**10%**
Total Sugars 6.6g	
Protein 28.9g	
Vitamin D 0mcg	0%
Calcium 32mg	2%
Iron 4mg	25%
Potassium 795mg	17%

Wild Boar

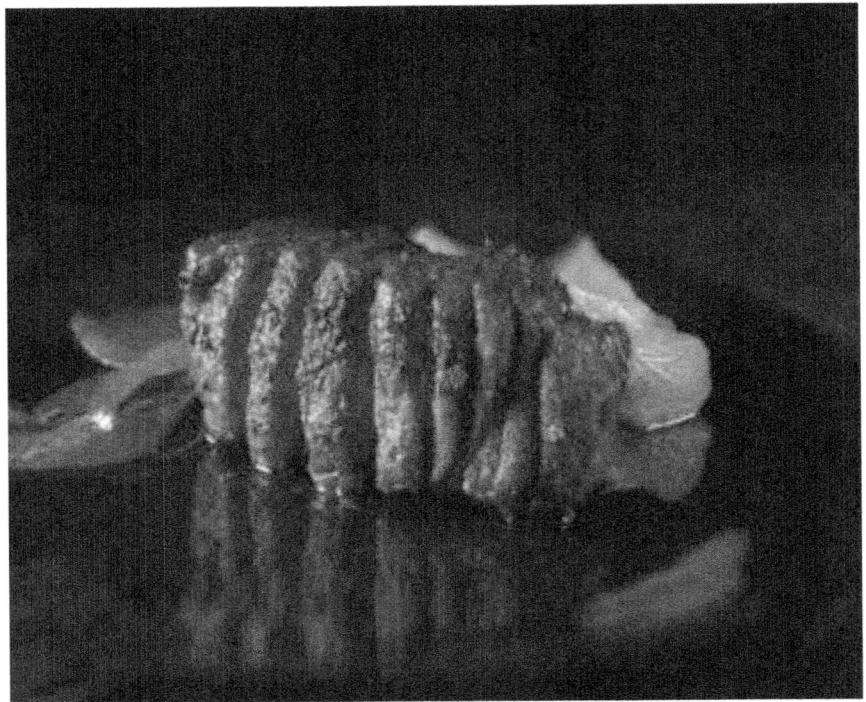

PREP TIME: 20 minutes
COOK TIME: 6 hours
SERVINGS: 4
Ingredients:
- 1 (4 pounds) wild boar roast
- 2 cups BBQ sauce

Marinade:
- 1 tbsp chopped fresh thyme
- 1/3 cup honey
- ¼ cup soy sauce

- ¼ tsp cayenne pepper
- ½ tsp oregano
- ¼ cup balsamic vinegar
- ½ tsp garlic powder
- 1 cup apple juice

Directions:
1. Combine all the marinade ingredients in a large mixing bowl. Pour the marinade into a zip-lock bag and add the boar. Massage the marinade into the boar roast. Refrigerate for 8 hours or overnight.
2. Remove the boar roast from the marinade and let it rest, until it comes to room temperature. Pat dry with paper towels.
3. Configure your wood pellet grill for indirect cooking and preheat the grill to 250°F, using apple hardwood pellets.
4. Place the boar roast on the grill and cook for 5-6 hours or until the internal temperature of the boar reaches 200°F.
5. Remove the boar from heat and let it sit until it is cool.
6. Pull the boar with 2 forks.
7. Heat up a large saucepan over medium to high heat. Add the BBQ sauce.

8. Add the shredded boar and cook for about 3 minutes, stirring often.
9. Remove the saucepan from heat.
10. Serve pulled boar and garnish with chopped fresh parsley.

Nutrition Facts
Servings: 4

Amount per serving
Calories 1044

% Daily Value*

Total Fat 20.4g	26%
Saturated Fat 6g	30%
Cholesterol 349mg	116%
Sodium 1936mg	84%
Total Carbohydrate 77.6g	28%
Dietary Fiber 1.3g	5%
Total Sugars 63g	
Protein 129.7g	
Vitamin D 0mcg	0%
Calcium 112mg	9%
Iron 6mg	36%
Potassium 2159mg	46%

Chapter Six

Other Recipes

Roasted Chickpeas Snacks

PREP TIME: 10 minutes
COOK TIME: 40 minutes
SERVINGS: 8
Ingredients:
- 1 15 ounces can chickpeas
- 1 tablespoon olive oil
- ¼ teaspoon freshly ground black pepper
- ½ teaspoon ground cumin

- ½ teaspoon smoked paprika
- ½ teaspoon onion powder
- ½ teaspoon garlic powder
- ½ teaspoon ground coriander
- ½ teaspoon sea salt or to taste

Directions:
1. Start your grill on smoke mode and leave the lid open for 5 minutes, until fire starts.
2. Close the lid and preheat grill to 450°F
3. Rinse and dry the chickpeas.
4. Spray a baking dish with a non-stick spray.
5. Pour the rinsed chickpeas into the baking dish and place the baking dish in the grill.
6. Place the baking dish on the grill and roast for 15 minutes.
7. While baking the chickpeas, combine the pepper, onion powder, garlic powder, cumin, paprika and sea salt in a medium bowl. Set aside.
8. After 15 minutes, bring out the baked chickpeas.
9. Trickle the olive oil over the chickpeas and stir until the chickpeas are all coated with oil.

10. Now, add the mixed spices and stir until the chickpeas are all coated with spices.
11. Place the coated chickpeas into the grill and roast for additional for 10 minutes.
12. Bring out the baking dish and stir the chickpeas again.
13. Return the chickpeas into the grill and bake for about 10 minutes or until the chickpeas are crispy.
14. Remove the baking sheet from the grill and let the chickpea cool for a few minutes.
15. Serve.

Nutrition Facts
Servings: 8

Amount per serving

Calories 211

	% Daily Value*
Total Fat 5g	6%
Saturated Fat 0.6g	3%
Cholesterol 0mg	0%
Sodium 130mg	6%
Total Carbohydrate 32.7g	12%
Dietary Fiber 9.4g	33%

Nutrition Facts
Servings: 8

Total Sugars 5.8g

Protein 10.4g

Vitamin D 0mcg	0%
Calcium 58mg	4%
Iron 3mg	19%
Potassium 475mg	10%

Glazed Carrots

PREP TIME: 15 minutes
COOK TIME: 30 minutes
SERVINGS: 4

Ingredients:
- 6 large carrots
- ½ teaspoon black pepper or to taste
- 2 tablespoons honey
- ½ teaspoon sea salt or taste
- 1 tablespoon extra-virgin olive oil

Garnish:
- Fresh chopped parsley or cilantro

Directions:
1. Wash and peel the carrots.
2. Cut the carrots into 1-inch slices.
3. In a medium bowl, combine the honey, olive oil, pepper and salt. Stir thoroughly until the ingredients are evenly mixed.
4. Pour the carrot into the honey mixture and stir until the carrot slices are all coated with honey mixture.
5. Spread the honey coated carrot slices on a sheet pan.
6. Start your grill on smoke mode and leave the lid open for 5 minutes, until fire starts.
7. Close the lid and preheat grill to 350°F
8. Place the sheet pan on the grill and roast for 20 minutes.

9. Remove the carrot from the grill and let it sit for a few minutes.
10. Garnish with chopped parsley and serve.

Nutrition Facts

Servings: 4

Amount per serving

Calories 107

% Daily Value*

Total Fat 3.5g	5%
Saturated Fat 0.5g	3%
Cholesterol 0mg	0%
Sodium 309mg	13%
Total Carbohydrate 19.4g	7%
Dietary Fiber 2.8g	10%
Total Sugars 13.9g	
Protein 1g	
Vitamin D 0mcg	0%
Calcium 37mg	3%
Iron 0mg	2%
Potassium 354mg	8%

Simple Roasted Butternut Squash

PREP TIME: 5 minutes
COOK TIME: 25 minutes
SERVINGS: 8
Ingredients:
- 1 (2 pounds) butternut squash
- 2 garlic cloves (minced)
- 2 tablespoon extra olive virgin oil
- 1 tsp paprika
- 1 tsp oregano
- 1 tsp thyme
- Salt and pepper to taste

Directions:

1. Start your grill on smoke mode and leave the grill open for 5 minutes, until fire Preheat the grill to 400°F.
2. Peel the butternut squash.
3. Cut the butternut squash into two (cut length wise).
4. Use a spoon to scoop out the seeds.
5. Cut the butternut squash into 1-inch chunks and wash the chunks with water.
6. In a big bowl, combine the butternut squash chunks and other ingredients.
7. Stir until the chunks are coated with the ingredients.
8. Spread the coated chunks on the sheet pan.
9. Place the sheet pan on the grill and bake for 25 minutes.
10. Remove the baked butternut squash from heat and let it sit to cool.
11. Serve.

Note: If you don't want to consume the butternut snacks immediately, leave it to cool and store in a tightly sealed container.

Nutrition Facts
Servings: 8

Amount per serving

Nutrition Facts

Servings: 8

Calories   83

	% Daily Value*
Total Fat 3.7g	5%
Saturated Fat 0.5g	3%
Cholesterol 0mg	0%
Sodium 331mg	14%
Total Carbohydrate 13.8g	5%
Dietary Fiber 2.6g	9%
Total Sugars 2.5g	
Protein 1.2g	
Vitamin D 0mcg	0%
Calcium 62mg	5%
Iron 1mg	7%
Potassium 413mg	9%

Spiced Nuts

PREP TIME: 5 minutes
COOK TIME: 20 minutes
SERVINGS: 32 tablespoons
Ingredients:
- 1 teaspoon dried rosemary
- 1/8 teaspoon cayenne pepper
- 1/8 teaspoon ground black pepper
- ½ teaspoon salt or to taste

- ½ teaspoon ground cumin
- 1 tablespoon olive oil
- 2 tablespoon maple syrup
- 2/3 cup raw and unsalted cashew nuts
- 2/3 cup raw and unsalted pecans
- 2/3 cup raw and unsalted walnuts

Directions:
1. Start your grill on smoke mode, leaving the lid opened for 5 minutes, or until fire starts.
2. Close the grill lid and preheat grill to 350°F.
3. In a large bowl, combine all the ingredients except the dried rosemary. Mix thoroughly until the ingredients are evenly mixed and all nuts are coated with spices.
4. Spread the spiced nuts on a baking sheet.
5. Place the baking sheet on the grill and roast the nuts for 20 to 25 minutes.
6. Remove the nuts from heat.
7. Sprinkle the dried rosemary on the nuts and stir to mix.
8. Leave the nuts to cool for a few minutes.
9. Serve and enjoy.

Nutrition Facts

Serving size: 1 tablespoon
Servings: 32

Amount per serving
Calories 64

% **Daily Value***

Total Fat 5.8g	7%
Saturated Fat 0.4g	2%
Cholesterol 0mg	0%
Sodium 35mg	2%
Total Carbohydrate 2.2g	1%
Dietary Fiber 0.6g	2%
Total Sugars 0.9g	
Protein 1.3g	
Vitamin D 0mcg	0%
Calcium 6mg	0%
Iron 0mg	1%
Potassium 4mg	0%

Grilled Potatoes

PREP TIME: 15 minutes
COOK TIME: 10 minutes
SERVINGS: 2
Ingredients:
- 2 medium russet potato (washed and scrubbed)
- 2 teaspoon olive oil
- 1 tsp Sea salt
- 1 tsp ground black pepper to taste
- ½ tsp cayenne pepper
- ½ tsp dried thyme
- ½ tsp dried oregano
- 1 tsp mustard powder

Directions:

1. Preheat the grill to 450°F with lid closed to 15 minutes.
2. Use a sharp knife to cut the potatoes into 1-inch thick round slices.
3. Mix the potato slices with olive oil. Add salt, ground pepper, cayenne, mustard, thyme and oregano. Toss to combine.
4. Adjust the grill to medium heat; arrange the potato slices into the grill and close the grill lid.
5. Cook on grill until one side of the potato slices turns golden brown. This will take about 5 minutes. Make sure you check constantly so the potatoes don't get burnt.
6. Flip the potatoes and cook until the other side of the potato slices turns golden brown too. This will take another 5 minutes.
7. Remove the potato slices from the grill and serve.

Nutrition Facts

Serving size: 1 tablespoon
Servings: 2

Amount per serving
Calories 222

Nutrition Facts

Serving size: 1 tablespoon
Servings: 2

	% Daily Value*
Total Fat 5.5g	7%
Saturated Fat 0.8g	4%
Cholesterol 0mg	0%
Sodium 961mg	42%
Total Carbohydrate 39g	14%
Dietary Fiber 4.9g	17%
Total Sugars 2.1g	
Protein 5.2g	
Vitamin D 0mcg	0%
Calcium 56mg	4%
Iron 3mg	16%
Potassium 993mg	21%

Eggplant Stuffed Lasagna

PREP TIME: 20 minutes
COOK TIME: 1 hour 5 minutes
SERVINGS: 12
Ingredients:

- 4 cups marinara sauce
- 1 large egg (beaten)
- 2 cups part-skim mozzarella cheese
- 2 large eggplants (sliced thinly)
- 2 tbsp olive oil
- 1 tsp salt or to taste
- 1 tsp ground black pepper or to taste

- ½ cup grated parmesan + 1 tbsp for sprinkling
- 2 cups part-skim ricotta cheese
- ½ tsp dried oregano
- 2 tsp Italian seasoning
- 2 tbsp freshly chopped parsley

Directions:
1. Preheat the wood pellet grill to 400°F with lid closed for 15 minutes.
2. Grease a baking sheet with parchment paper.
3. Brush both sides of the eggplant slices with olive oil and season them with little salt and pepper.
4. Arrange the eggplant slices into the baking sheet in a single layer.
5. Place the baking sheet on the grill and bake for about 15 minutes or until the eggplant slices are tender and golden brown.
6. Remove the eggplant slices from the grill and reduce the heat to 375°F.
7. In a mixing bowl, combine the ricotta cheese, ½ cup parmesan and egg. Mix until the ingredients are well combined.

8. In another mixing bowl, combine the marinara, Italian seasoning, oregano, salt and pepper. Mix until well combined.
9. Pour some of the marinara mixture into the bottom of a cash iron baking pan.
10. Layer about 5 eggplant slices over the sauce mixture in a single layer.
11. Pour some of the cheese-egg mixture over it. Sprinkle some mozzarella cheese over it.
12. Layer another 5 eggplant slices over the mixture and repeat step 9.
13. Repeat the process until you have assembled all the ingredients.
14. Finally, top with remaining sauce, mozzarella and 1 tbsp parmesan.
15. Cover the casserole dish with aluminum foil and place it on the grill. Cook at 375°F for 40 minutes.
16. Remove the dish from the grill and uncover it. Return it to the grill and cook for additional 10 minutes.
17. Remove the lasagna from the grill and let it sit for a few minutes to cool
18. Serve and garnish with chopped fresh basil.

Nutrition Facts

Servings: 12

Amount per serving

Calories 205

% Daily Value*

Total Fat 10.4g	**13%**
Saturated Fat 4.2g	**21%**
Cholesterol 36mg	**12%**
Sodium 662mg	**29%**
Total Carbohydrate 18.7g	**7%**
Dietary Fiber 5g	**18%**
Total Sugars 9.9g	
Protein 10.2g	
Vitamin D 1mcg	7%
Calcium 183mg	14%
Iron 1mg	7%
Potassium 503mg	11%

Chicken Quesadilla

PREP TIME: 10 minutes
COOK TIME: 10 minutes
SERVINGS: 2
Ingredients:
- 1 tbsp olive oil
- 1 cup shredded chicken
- 1/8 tsp garlic powder
- 1/8 tsp dried basil
- 1/8 tsp crushed pepper
- 1 red bell pepper (chopped)
- 2 roma tomatoes (diced)

- 1 small onion (chopped)
- 1 ½ cup mozzarella cheese
- 1 ½ cups cheddar cheese

Directions:
1. Place a cast iron skillet in the wood pellet grill and preheat the grill to 400°F with lid closed for 15 minutes.
2. Add the oil to the skillet.
3. Once the oil is hot, add the onion, tomatoes and red bell pepper. Cook until the veggies are tender. Add the shredded chicken, salt, basil, crushed pepper and garlic powder. Stir to combine.
4. Remove the skillet from heat.
5. Line a cast iron pizza pan with parchment paper. Combine the mozzarella cheese and cheddar cheese. Spread the cheese into the pizza pan and shape into a circle.
6. Place the pizza pan on the grill and cook for 5 minutes all until the cheese is melted.
7. Remove the pizza pan from heat and drain excess oil.
8. Add the shredded chicken and veggies to one half of the cheese crust.

9. Use the parchment paper to fold the cheese crust such that the chicken-veggie filling will be in the middle.
10. Return the pan to the grill and bake for 5 minutes.
11. Remove the quesadilla from the grill.
12. Serve warm and enjoy.

Nutrition Facts

Serving size: 1 tablespoon
Servings: 2

Amount per serving

Calories 623

% Daily Value*

Total Fat 41.4g	**53%**
Saturated Fat 21.8g	**109%**
Cholesterol 154mg	**51%**
Sodium 707mg	**31%**
Total Carbohydrate 14.5g	**5%**
Dietary Fiber 3.1g	**11%**
Total Sugars 8.2g	
Protein 49.5g	
Vitamin D 10mcg	51%
Calcium 661mg	51%

Nutrition Facts

Serving size: 1 tablespoon
Servings: 2

Iron 2mg	10%
Potassium 671mg	14%

Buffalo Chicken Meatballs

PREP TIME: 10 minutes
COOK TIME: 15 minutes
SERVINGS: 10 meatballs
Ingredients:
- 1 pound ground chicken
- 1 egg (beaten)
- 1 garlic clove (minced)
- 2 tbsp melted butter
- 1/2 cup hot sauce
- 1/3 cup almond flour
- 4 tbsp grated cheddar cheese
- ½ tsp onion powder
- ½ tsp oregano

- 1 tbsp freshly chopped parsley
- 1 tbsp ranch dressing or more for serving

Directions:
1. Start your grill on smoke mode and leave the lid opened for 5 minutes, or until fire starts.
2. Close the lid and preheat the wood pellet grill to 450°F for 15 minutes. Use hickory hardwood pellets
3. Grease a baking sheet.
4. In a large mixing bowl, combine the onion powder, hot sauce, ground chicken, egg, butter, almond flour, cheese and garlic. Mix until the ingredients are well combined.
5. Mold the mixture into balls and arrange the balls into the baking sheet in a single layer.
6. Place the baking sheet on the grill and smoke for about 15 minutes or until the internal temperature of the meatball reaches 165°F.
7. Remove the meatballs from the grill and let them cool for a few minutes.
8. Serve and top with chopped parsley and ranch dressing.

Nutrition Facts
Servings: 10

Amount per serving
Calories 150

% Daily Value*

Total Fat 8.9g	**11%**
Saturated Fat 3.3g	**16%**
Cholesterol 66mg	**22%**
Sodium 394mg	**17%**
Total Carbohydrate 1.4g	**1%**
Dietary Fiber 0.5g	**2%**
Total Sugars 0.3g	
Protein 15.3g	
Vitamin D 3mcg	17%
Calcium 34mg	3%
Iron 1mg	4%
Potassium 142mg	3%

Cauliflower Hash Browns

PREP TIME: 15 minutes
COOK TIME: 25 minutes
SERVINGS: 6
Ingredients:
- ¼ cup real bacon bits
- 1 large egg
- 1 cup shredded cheddar cheese
- 3 cups grated cauliflower
- ½ tsp chili powder
- 1/8 tsp ground black pepper
- ½ tsp salt
- 1tbsp chopped green onions

Directions:

1. Preheat the pellet grill to 400°F with lid closed for 15 minutes.
2. Roll the cauliflower into a clean dish towel and squeeze hard to remove moisture from the grated cauliflower.
3. Combine the cauliflower and cheddar cheese in a large mixing bowl.
4. Pour in the egg and add the bacon bits, salt, black pepper, green onions and chili powder. Stir thoroughly until the ingredients are evenly combined.
5. Spray a baking sheet with non-sticky cooking spray.
6. Divide the cauliflower mixture into six equal portions and place each portion on the baking sheet.
7. Press down each portion with a flat bottom neat glass cup. This will flatten the portions.
8. Use your hand or a knife to shape each flattened portion to oval.
9. Place the baking sheet on the grill and cook for about 15 minutes or until browned.
10. Remove the baking sheet from the grill and leave the hash browns to cool for a few minutes.

11. Serve and enjoy.

Nutrition Facts

Servings: 6

Amount per serving
Calories 101

	% Daily Value*
Total Fat 7.2g	9%
Saturated Fat 4.3g	21%
Cholesterol 51mg	17%
Sodium 340mg	15%
Total Carbohydrate 3.2g	1%
Dietary Fiber 1.4g	5%
Total Sugars 1.4g	
Protein 6.8g	
Vitamin D 5mcg	26%
Calcium 153mg	12%
Iron 1mg	3%
Potassium 189mg	4%

Smoked Carrot Fries

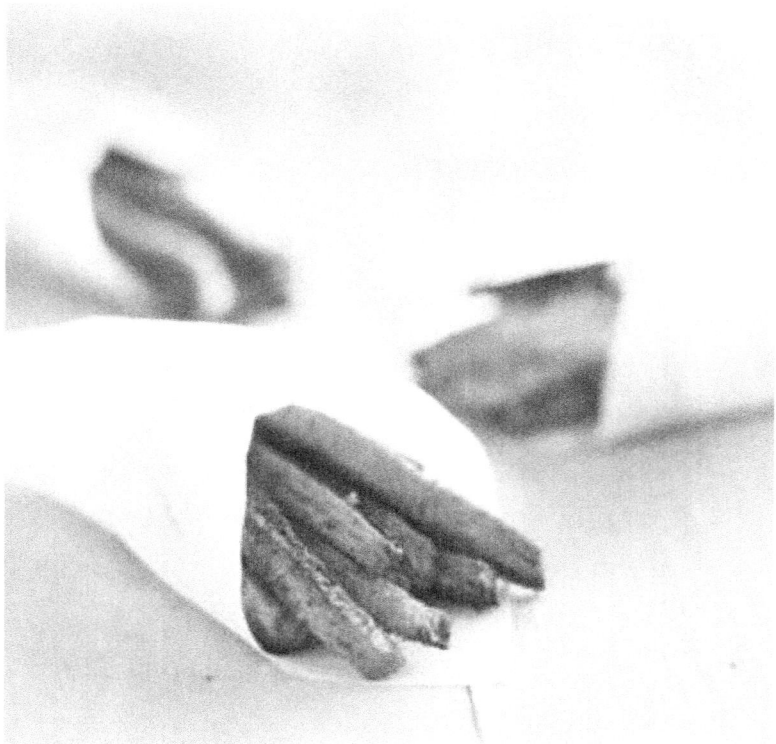

PREP TIME: 15 minutes
COOK TIME: 20 minutes
SERVINGS: 3
Ingredients:
- 1 pound carrots (washed)
- ½ tsp thyme
- ½ tsp onion powder
- ½ tsp black pepper or to taste
- 2 tbsp olive oil

- 2 tbsp tapioca flour
- 1 tsp sea salt
- ½ tsp garlic powder

Directions:
1. Start your grill on smoke mode and leave the lid open for 5 minutes, or until fire starts.
2. Close the lid and preheat grill to 450°F with lid closed for 15 minutes.
3. Peel the carrots and cut each carrot into four (cut lengthwise).
4. In a medium mixing bowl, mix the thyme, onion powder, tapioca flour, garlic powder, black pepper and salt.
5. Toss the carrots into the mixed ingredients. Mix until the carrot slices are all coated with seasoning.
6. Add 1 ½ tbsp olive oil and mix thoroughly.
7. Grease a baking sheet with a non-stick cooking spray and arrange the carrot slices into the baking sheet in a single layer.
8. Place the baking sheet in the grill and smoke for about 20 minutes or until the carrot slices are tender and crispy. Flip the carrot slices after the first 10 minutes.

9. Remove the baking sheet from the grill and let the carrots to cool.
10. Serve and sprinkle with the remaining ½ tbsp olive oil.

Nutrition Facts

Servings: 3

Amount per serving
Calories 165

% Daily Value*

Total Fat 9.4g	**12%**
Saturated Fat 1.3g	**7%**
Cholesterol 0mg	**0%**
Sodium 729mg	**32%**
Total Carbohydrate 20.4g	**7%**
Dietary Fiber 4g	**14%**
Total Sugars 7.7g	
Protein 1.4g	
Vitamin D 0mcg	0%
Calcium 56mg	4%
Iron 1mg	4%
Potassium 498mg	11%

Empanadas

PREP TIME: 20 minutes
COOK TIME: 20 minutes
SERVINGS: 4
Ingredients:
- 3/4 cup + 1 tbsp all-purpose flour
- ½ tsp baking powder
- 1 tbsp sugar
- ¼ tsp salt or to taste
- 2 tbsp cold water
- 1/3 cups butter
- 1 small egg (beaten)

Filling:
- ½ small onion (chopped)
- 57 g ground beef (1/8 pound)

- 2 tbsp marinara sauce
- 1 small carrot peeled and diced)
- 1/8 small potato (peeled and diced) 35 grams
- 2 tbsp water
- 1 garlic clove (minced)
- 1 tbsp olive oil
- 1 tbsp raisin
- 2 tbsp green peas
- ½ tsp salt or taste
- 1/2 tsp ground black pepper or to taste
- 1 hard-boiled egg (sliced)

Directions:
1. Start your grill on smoke mode and leave the lid opened for 5 minutes, or until fire starts.
2. Close the grill and preheat grill to 400°F with lid closed for 15 minutes, using hickory hardwood pellets.
3. For the fillet, place a cast iron skillet on the grill and add the oil.
4. Once the oil is hot, add the onion and garlic and sauté until the onion is tender and translucent.
5. Add the ground beef and sauté until it is tender, stirring often.

6. Stir in the marinara, salt, water and pepper.
7. Bring to a boil and reduce the heat. Cook for 30 seconds.
8. Stir in the carrot, raisin and potatoes and cook for 3 minutes.
9. Stir in the green peas and sliced egg. Cook for additional 2 minutes, stirring often.
10. Spray a baking dish with a non-stick spray.
11. For the dough, combine the flour, baking powder salt and sugar in a large mixing bowl. Mix until well combined.
12. Add butter and mix until it is well incorporated.
13. Add egg and mix until you form dough.
14. Put the dough on a flour surface and knead the dough for a few minutes. Add more flour if the dough is not thick enough.
15. Roll the dough flat with a rolling pin. The flat dough should be ¼ inch thick.
16. Cut the flat dough into circles.
17. Add equal amounts of the beef mixture to the middle of each flat circular dough slice. Fold the dough slice and close the edges by pressing with your fingers or a fork.
18. Arrange the empanadas into the baking sheet in a single layer.

19. Place the baking sheet on the grill and bake for 10 minutes.
20. Remove the baking sheet from the grill and flip the empanadas.
21. Bake for another 10 minutes on the grill or until empanadas are golden brown.

Nutrition Facts
Servings: 4

Amount per serving
Calories 353

% Daily Value*

Total Fat 22.3g	**29%**
Saturated Fat 11.3g	**56%**
Cholesterol 129mg	**43%**
Sodium 481mg	**21%**
Total Carbohydrate 28.9g	**10%**
Dietary Fiber 1.9g	**7%**
Total Sugars 6.6g	
Protein 10.4g	
Vitamin D 18mcg	88%
Calcium 60mg	5%
Iron 5mg	25%
Potassium 327mg	7%

Mango Bread

PREP TIME: 15 minutes
COOK TIME: 60 minutes
SERVINGS: 4
Ingredients:
- 2 ½ cup cubed ripe mangoes
- 2 cups all-purpose flour
- 1 tsp baking powder
- 1 tsp baking soda
- 2 eggs (beaten)
- 1 tsp cinnamon
- 1 tsp vanilla extract
- ½ tsp nutmeg
- ¾ cup olive oil

- ¾ cup sugar
- 1 tbsp lemon juice
- ½ tsp salt
- ½ cup chopped dates

Directions:
1. Start your grill on smoke mode and leave the lip opened for 5 minutes, or until fire starts.
2. Close the lid and preheat the grill to 350°F for 15 minutes, using alder hardwood pellets.
3. Grease an 8 by 4-inch loaf pan.
4. In a mixing bowl, combine the flour, baking powder, baking soda, cinnamon, salt and sugar.
5. In another mixing bowl, whisk together the egg, lemon juice, oil and vanilla.
6. Pour the egg mixture into the flour mixture and mix until you well combined.
7. Fold in the mangoes and dates.
8. Pour the mixture into the loaf pan and place the pan in the grill.
9. Place the loaf pan directly on the grill bake for about 50 to 60 minutes or until a toothpick inserted in the middle of the bread comes out clean.

10. After the baking cycle, remove the loaf pan from the grill and transfer the bread to a wire rack to cool completely.
11. Slice and serve.

Nutrition Facts
Servings: 4

Amount per serving	
Calories	**856**
	% Daily Value*
Total Fat 41.2g	**53%**
Saturated Fat 6.4g	**32%**
Cholesterol 82mg	**27%**
Sodium 641mg	**28%**
Total Carbohydrate 118.9g	**43%**
Dietary Fiber 5.5g	**20%**
Total Sugars 66.3g	
Protein 10.7g	
Vitamin D 8mcg	39%
Calcium 102mg	8%
Iron 4mg	22%
Potassium 552mg	12%

Kid-friendly Zucchini Bread

PREP TIME: 15 minutes
COOK TIME: 50 minutes
SERVINGS: 8 slices (4 servings)
Ingredients:
- 1 ½ cup whole wheat flour
- 2 eggs
- 1 tsp salt
- 1 tsp baking powder
- 1 tsp baking soda
- ½ cup maple syrup
- 4 tbsp butter (melted)
- 2 tsp cinnamon
- 2 tsp vanilla extract
- 1 ½ cups shredded zucchini
- 2 tbsp lemon juice
- 1 tsp ground nutmeg

Directions:
1. Start your grill on smoke mode and leave the lip opened for 5 minutes, or until fire starts.
2. Close the lid and preheat the grill to 350°F for 15 minutes, using apple hardwood pellets.
3. Wrap the shredded zucchini with a clean kitchen towel and squeeze to remove excess liquid. Set aside.
4. In a mixing bowl, whisk together the eggs, maple syrup, butter, vanilla extract and lemon juice.
5. In a large mixing bowl, mix together the flour, baking soda, baking powder, nutmeg, cinnamon and salt.
6. Pour the egg mixture into the flour mixture and mix until the ingredients are well combined.
7. Fold in the shredded zucchini.
8. Pour the batter into the prepared loaf pan and spread it to the edges of the pan.
9. Place the loaf pan directly on the grill and bake for about 50 minutes or until a toothpick inserted in the middle of the bread comes out clean.
10. Remove the loaf pan from the grill and transfer the bread to a wire rack to cool.
11. Serve and enjoy.

Nutrition Facts
Servings: 4

Amount per serving
Calories 428

% **Daily Value***

Total Fat 14.6g	**19%**
Saturated Fat 8.3g	**41%**
Cholesterol 112mg	**37%**
Sodium 1020mg	**44%**
Total Carbohydrate 66g	**24%**
Dietary Fiber 2.5g	**9%**
Total Sugars 25.1g	
Protein 8.4g	
Vitamin D 16mcg	78%
Calcium 123mg	9%
Iron 3mg	19%
Potassium 420mg	9%

Grill Baked Shrimp

PREP TIME: 35 minutes
COOK TIME: 10 minutes
SERVINGS: 4
Ingredients:
- 12 large shrimps (peeled and vein removed)
- 2 tbsp butter (softened)
- 1tsp garlic
- 4 tbsp parmesan cheese
- ½ tsp sea salt or to taste
- ½ tsp ground black pepper
- 6 tbsp almond flour or coconut flour
- 2 tbsp olive oil
  Garnish:
- Fresh chopped parsley

Directions:
13. Combine the garlic, salt, pepper and olive oil in a large mixing bowl.
14. Add the shrimps and toss until the shrimps are all coated.
15. Cover the mixing bowl and place it in the fridge. Refrigerate for about 30 minutes.
16. Meanwhile, preheat the grill to 245°C.
17. Line a baking sheet with parchment paper. Set aside.
18. In another mixing bowl, mix the almond flour and cheese.
19. Add the marinated shrimps to the flour-cheese mixture and toss until the shrimps are all coated.
20. Arrange the shrimps into the lined baking sheet in a single layer.
21. Place the baking sheet in the preheated grill and until the shrimps are crispy. This will take about 10- 12 minutes.
22. After the baking circle, remove the baking sheet from the grill and leave the shrimps to cool for a few minutes.
23. Serve and garnish with chopped fresh parsley and serve.

Nutrition Facts
Servings: 4

Amount per serving
Calories 222

% Daily Value*

Total Fat 20.3g	**26%**
Saturated Fat 6.4g	**32%**
Cholesterol 57mg	**19%**
Sodium 401mg	**17%**
Total Carbohydrate 3.2g	**1%**
Dietary Fiber 1.2g	**4%**
Total Sugars 0.4g	
Protein 9.1g	
Vitamin D 4mcg	20%
Calcium 124mg	10%
Iron 1mg	3%
Potassium 36mg	1%

Mozzarella Meatballs

PREP TIME: 10 minutes
COOK TIME: 20 minutes
SERVINGS: 4
Ingredients:
- 4 tbsp tomato paste
- 2 large eggs (beaten)
- 1 tsp Worcestershire sauce
- 1 tsp salt or to taste
- ½ pound ground beef (75% lean)
- 1 tsp oregano
- 1 tsp Italian seasoning
- ½ cup mozzarella cheese
- ½ cup black olives
- 2 large onions (finely chopped)

- 2 tbsp minced fresh basil
- 4 garlic cloves (minced)
- 2 tbsp flaxseed
- 1 tsp ground black pepper or to taste

Garnish:
- 2 tbsp chopped fresh parsley

Directions:
1. Start your grill on smoke mode and leave the lid opened for 5 minutes, or until fire starts.
2. Close the lid and preheat the wood pellet grill to 400°F for 15 minutes. Use hickory hardwood pellets
3. Grease a baking sheet.
4. In a large mixing bowl, combine all the ingredients.
5. Mix thoroughly until the ingredients are well combined.
6. Mold the ingredients into meatballs and arrange the meatballs into the baking sheet.
7. Place the baking sheet on the grill and smoke for about 20 minutes, until the meatballs are done.

8. Remove the baking sheet from the grill and leave the meatballs to cool for a few minutes.
9. Serve and garnish with fresh chopped parsley.

Nutrition Facts

Serving size: 1 tablespoon
Servings: 4

Amount per serving
Calories 244

	% Daily Value*
Total Fat 10.1g	13%
Saturated Fat 3g	15%
Cholesterol 146mg	49%
Sodium 856mg	37%
Total Carbohydrate 14.4g	5%
Dietary Fiber 4.1g	15%
Total Sugars 5.8g	
Protein 24g	
Vitamin D 9mcg	44%
Calcium 72mg	6%
Iron 14mg	76%
Potassium 593mg	13%

BBQ Pork Rinds

PREP TIME: 3 minutes
COOK TIME: 5 minutes
SERVINGS: 4
Ingredients:
- 3.75 oz bag of pork rinds
- ¼ tsp Italian seasoning
- ½ tsp ground black pepper
- ½ tsp onion powder
- ¼ tsp dried oregano
- 1 tsp dried paprika
- 1 tsp salt

Directions:

1. Preheat the grill to to 350°F with lid closed for 15 minutes, using apple hardwood pellets.
2. In a large mixing bowl, combine the chili, salt, Italian seasoning, onion powder, oregano, paprika and black pepper.
3. Arrange the pork rinds into a greased baking sheet on a single layer.
4. Place the baking sheet on the grill and bake for about 5 minutes.
5. Bring out the baking sheet and toss the rinds into the bowl containing the mixed seasonings.
6. Stir thoroughly until the rinds are all coated.
7. Serve and enjoy.

Nutrition Facts
Servings: 6

Amount per serving
Calories 26

	% Daily Value*
Total Fat 1.5g	2%
Saturated Fat 0.6g	3%
Cholesterol 5mg	2%
Sodium 519mg	23%

Nutrition Facts

Servings: 6

Total Carbohydrate 0.5g	**0%**
Dietary Fiber 0.2g	**1%**
Total Sugars 0.1g	
Protein 2.8g	
Vitamin D 0mcg	0%
Calcium 7mg	1%
Iron 0mg	1%
Potassium 14mg	0%

Chicken Parmesan

PREP TIME: 10 minutes

COOK TIME: 25 minutes
SERVINGS: 4
Ingredients:
- 4 thin slices chicken breast
- 1 cup grated mozzarella cheese
- 2 large eggs
- 2 cups finely crushed pork rind
- ½ tsp onion powder
- ½ cup marinara
- ½ cup powdered parmesan
- 1 tsp garlic powder
- 1 tsp seasoning salt
- ½ tsp paprika

Garnish:
- Chopped fresh parsley

Directions:
1. Preheat the grill to 350°5 with lid closed for 15 minutes.
2. Grease a large cookie sheet.
3. In a mixing bowl, mix the pork rind, seasoning salt, paprika, pepper, garlic powder, onion powder and parmesan.
4. Break the eggs into another mixing bowl and whisk.

5. Pick each of the chicken breast slices and dip it into the egg mixture and then the pork rind mixture. Make sure each chicken breast slice is well coated.
6. Arrange the coated chicken breast slices into the greased cookie sheet.
7. Place the cookie sheet on the grill and bake for about 15 to 20 minutes.
8. Remove the baking sheet from the grill and spread the marinara over the chicken.
9. Top with mozzarella cheese and return the cookie sheet to the grill.
10. Cook until cheese melts.
11. Remove the chicken from the grill.
12. Serve and garnish with chopped fresh parsley.

Nutrition Facts

Servings: 4

Amount per serving

Calories   **548**

	% Daily Value*
Total Fat 28.3g	36%
Saturated Fat 11.4g	57%
Cholesterol 235mg	78%

Nutrition Facts

Servings: 4

Sodium 1786mg	**78%**
Total Carbohydrate 4g	**1%**
Dietary Fiber 0.2g	**1%**
Total Sugars 0.5g	
Protein 69.5g	
Vitamin D 9mcg	44%
Calcium 132mg	10%
Iron 1mg	8%
Potassium 50mg	1%

Beef and Bacon Casserole

PREP TIME: 20 minutes

COOK TIME: 45 minutes
SERVINGS: 8
Ingredients:
- 2 tbsp olive oil
- 12 large eggs
- 1 tsp pepper
- 1 tsp seasoning salt
- ¼ cup chopped green onions
- 1 tsp paprika
- 1 small sweet onion (diced)
- 1 small green pepper (chopped)
- ¾ cups green beans
- 1 pound ground beef
- 1 cup heavy cream
- 1 pound shredded cheddar cheese

Directions:
1. Preheat the grill to 350°F with lid closed for 15 minutes
2. Spray 9 by 13 inch cast iron pan with cooking spray.
3. Heat up the olive oil in a large nonstick skillet over medium-high heat.
4. Add the green beans, onions, paprika, green onions and green pepper.

5. Stir fry for about five minutes until the vegetables are tender and the onion is browned.
6. Add the ground beef and break it apart with a wooden spoon. Cook until the ground beef is cooked. Stir constantly.
7. Break the eggs into a large mixing bowl and beat.
8. Add the heavy cream, salt and pepper. Whisk thoroughly to combine.
9. Add about ¾ of the cheese to the egg mixture and mix until well combined.
10. Stir in the cooked ground beef and vegetables.
11. Pour the mixture into the prepared baking pan.
12. Sprinkle the remaining cheese over the casserole mixture.
13. Place the pan in the preheated grill and bake for about 45 minutes or until the eggs are fully set and the casserole top turns golden brown.
14. Remove the baking pan from the grill and leave the casserole to cool for a few minutes.

15. Serve and enjoy.

Nutrition Facts
Servings: 8

Amount per serving
Calories 534

% Daily Value*

Total Fat 38.9g	**50%**
Saturated Fat 19.6g	**98%**
Cholesterol 410mg	**137%**
Sodium 793mg	**34%**
Total Carbohydrate 4.3g	**2%**
Dietary Fiber 1g	**3%**
Total Sugars 1.7g	
Protein 41.6g	
Vitamin D 41mcg	204%
Calcium 470mg	36%
Iron 13mg	71%
Potassium 464mg	10%

Keto Quiche

PREP TIME: 10 minutes
COOK TIME: 45 minutes
SERVINGS: 6
Ingredients:

- 12 tbsp unsalted butter (soften)
- 12 large eggs
- 8 ounces grated cheddar cheese (divided)
- 4 ounces cream cheese
- ½ tsp salt or to taste
- ½ tsp ground black pepper or to taste
- 1 yellow onion (diced)
- 1 green bell pepper (chopped)
- 3 cups broccoli florets (chopped)
- 1 tbsp olive oil

Directions:
1. Preheat the grill to 325°F with lid closed for 15 minutes.
2. Heat up the olive oil in a skillet over high heat.
3. Add the chopped onion, broccoli and green pepper. Cook for about 8 minutes, stirring constantly.
4. Remove the skillet from heat.
5. Process the egg and cheese in a food processor, adding the melted butter in bit while processing.
6. Combine 4ounce grated cheddar cheese, salt and pepper in a quiche pan.
7. Toss the cooked vegetable into the pan and mix.
8. Pour the egg mixture over the ingredients in the quiche pan.
9. Sprinkle the remaining grated cheese over it.
10. Place the pan in the preheated grill and bake for 45 minutes.
11. Remove and transfer the quiche to a rack to cool.
12. Slice and serve.

Nutrition Facts

Servings: 6

Amount per serving

Calories 615

% Daily Value*

Total Fat 54.7g	**70%**
Saturated Fat 30.1g	**151%**
Cholesterol 494mg	**165%**
Sodium 804mg	**35%**
Total Carbohydrate 8.1g	**3%**
Dietary Fiber 1.9g	**7%**
Total Sugars 3.6g	
Protein 25.4g	
Vitamin D 55mcg	277%
Calcium 376mg	29%
Iron 3mg	16%
Potassium 411mg	9%

Breakfast Sausage Casserole

PREP TIME: 15 minutes
COOK TIME: 30 minutes
SERVINGS: 6
Ingredients:
- 1 pound ground sausage
- 1 tsp ground sage
- ¼ cup green beans (chopped)
- 2 tsp yellow mustard
- 1 tsp cayenne
- 8 tbsp mayonnaise
- 1 large onion (diced)
- 2 cups diced zucchini

- 2 cups shredded cabbage
- 1 ½ cup shredded cheddar cheese
- Chopped fresh parsley to taste

Directions:
1. Preheat the grill to 360°F and grease a cast iron casserole dish.
2. Heat up a large skillet over medium to high heat.
3. Toss the sausage into the skillet, break it apart and cook until browned, stirring constantly.
4. Add the cabbage, zucchini, green beans and onion and cook until the vegetables are tender, stirring frequently.
5. Pour the cooked sausage and vegetable into the casserole dish and spread it.
6. Break the eggs into a mixing bowl and add the mustard, cayenne, mayonnaise and sage. Whish until well combined.
7. Stir in half of the cheddar cheese.
8. Pour the egg mixture over the ingredients in the casserole dish.
9. Sprinkle with the remaining shredded cheese.

10. Place the baking dish on the grill and bake for 30 minutes or until the top of the casserole turns golden brown.
11. Garnish with chopped fresh parsley.

Nutrition Facts

Servings: 6

Amount per serving

Calories 472

% Daily Value*

Total Fat 37.6g	**48%**
Saturated Fat 13.9g	**69%**
Cholesterol 98mg	**33%**
Sodium 909mg	**40%**
Total Carbohydrate 10.7g	**4%**
Dietary Fiber 1.9g	**7%**
Total Sugars 4g	
Protein 23.1g	
Vitamin D 3mcg	17%
Calcium 242mg	19%
Iron 2mg	9%
Potassium 446mg	9%

Crunchy Avocado Fries

PREP TIME: 15 Minutes
COOK TIME: 25 Minutes
SERVINGS: 3
Ingredients:
- 1/3 cup nutritional yeast
- 2 tbsp tapioca flour
- ½ tsp garlic powder
- 1 avocado (peeled)
- ½ tsp ground black pepper
- ¼ tsp sea salt
- 2 tbsp almond milk

Directions:
1. Preheat the grill to 360°F with lid closed for 10-15 minutes.

2. Grease a baking sheet
3. Cut the avocado into 12 pieces (cut lengthwise). Set aside.
4. In a small mixing bowl, combine the garlic powder, black pepper, flour and salt. Set aside.
5. Put the milk in a separate bowl and the yeast in a separate bowl as well.
6. Use a fork to pick one avocado slice; dip it into the flour mixture; dip it into the milk and then the yeast.
7. Drop the coated avocado slice in the parchment paper lined baking dish.
8. Repeat step 5 and 6 for the remaining avocado slices.
9. Ensure that the avocado slices are not stacked over each other.
10. Place the baking sheet in the preheated grill and bake until the coated avocado slices turn golden brown. This will take about 23-25 minutes.
11. Remove the baking sheet from the grill and let the avocado slices cool for a few minutes.
12. Serve and enjoy.

Nutrition Facts
Servings: 3

Amount per serving
Calories 233

% Daily Value*

Total Fat 16.4g	**21%**
Saturated Fat 5g	**25%**
Cholesterol 0mg	**0%**
Sodium 172mg	**7%**
Total Carbohydrate 17.2g	**6%**
Dietary Fiber 9.3g	**33%**
Total Sugars 0.8g	
Protein 9.8g	
Vitamin D 0mcg	0%
Calcium 25mg	2%
Iron 4mg	24%
Potassium 787mg	17%

Low Carb Almond Flour Bread

PREP TIME: 10 minutes
COOK TIME: 1 hour 15 minutes
SERVINGS: 24 slices
Ingredients:
- 1 tsp sea salt or to taste
- 1 tbsp apple cider vinegar
- ½ cup warm water
- ¼ cup coconut oil
- 4 large eggs (beaten)
- 1 tbsp gluten free baking powder
- 2 cup blanched almond flour
- ¼ cup Psyllium husk powder

- 1 tsp ginger (optional)

Directions:
1. Preheat the grill to 350°F with lid closed for 15 minutes
2. Line a 9 by 5 inch loaf pan with parchment paper. Set aside.
3. Combine the ginger, Psyllium husk powder, almond flour, salt, baking powder in a large mixing bowl.
4. In another mixing bowl, mix the coconut oil, apple cider vinegar, eggs and warm water. Mix thoroughly.
5. Gradually pour the flour mixture into the egg mixture, stirring as you pour. Stir until it forms a smooth batter.
6. Fill the lined loaf pan with the batter and cover the batter with aluminum foil.
7. Place the loaf pan directly on the grill and bake for about 1 hour or until a toothpick or knife inserted in the middle of the bread comes out clean.

Nutrition Facts
Servings: 24

Amount per serving

Nutrition Facts

Servings: 24

Calories   93

	% Daily Value*
Total Fat 7.5g	10%
Saturated Fat 2.6g	13%
Cholesterol 31mg	10%
Sodium 139mg	6%
Total Carbohydrate 3.6g	1%
Dietary Fiber 2.2g	8%
Total Sugars 0.1g	
Protein 3.1g	
Vitamin D 3mcg	15%
Calcium 92mg	7%
Iron 0mg	1%
Potassium 13mg	0%

Rosemary Cheese Breadstick

PREP TIME: 10 minutes
COOK TIME: 12 minutes
SERVINGS: 30 Breadstick
Ingredients:
- 1 ½ cup sunflower seeds
- ½ tsp sea salt
- 1 egg
- 1 tsp fresh rosemary (finely chopped)
- 2 tsp xanthan gum
- 2 tbsp cream cheese
- 2 cups grated mozzarella

Directions:

1. Preheat the grill to 400°F with lid closed for 15 minutes.
2. Toss the sunflower seeds into a powerful blender and blend until it smooth and flour-like.
3. Transfer the sunflower seed flour into a mixing bowl and add the rosemary and xanthan gum. Mix and set aside.
4. Melt the cheese in a microwave. To do this, combine the cream cheese and mozzarella cheese in a microwave safe dish.
5. Place the microwave safe dish in the grill and heat the cheese on high for 1 minute.
6. Bring out the dish and stir. Place the dish in the grill and heat for 30 seconds. Bring out the dish and stir until smooth.
7. Pour the melted cheese into a large mixing bowl.
8. Add the sunflower flour mixture to the melted cheese and stir the ingredients are well combined.
9. Add the salt and egg and mix thoroughly to form smooth dough.
10. Measure out equal pieces of the dough and roll into sticks.

11. Grease a baking sheet with oil and arrange the breadsticks into the baking sheet in a single layer.
12. Use the back of a knife or metal spoon to make lines on the breadsticks.
13. Place the baking sheet on the grill and make for about 12 minutes or until the breadsticks turn golden brown.
14. Remove the baking sheet from the grill and let the breadsticks cool for a few minutes.
15. Serve.

Nutrition Facts
Servings: 30

Amount per serving
Calories 23

	% Daily Value*
Total Fat 1.9g	2%
Saturated Fat 0.5g	3%
Cholesterol 7mg	2%
Sodium 47mg	2%
Total Carbohydrate 0.6g	0%
Dietary Fiber 0.2g	1%
Total Sugars 0.1g	

Nutrition Facts
Servings: 30

Protein 1.2g

Vitamin D 1mcg	3%
Calcium 5mg	0%
Iron 0mg	1%
Potassium 18mg	0%

Cinnamon Almond Shortbread

PREP TIME: 20 minutes
COOK TIME: 20 minutes
SERVINGS: 16

Ingredients:
- 2 tsp cinnamon
- ½ cup unsalted butter (softened)
- 1 large egg (beaten)
- ½ tsp salt or to taste
- 2 cups almond flour
- ¼ cup sugar
- 1 tsp ginger (optional)

Directions:
1. Preheat the grill to 300°F with lid closed for 5 minutes.
2. Grease a cookie sheet with oil.
3. In a large bowl, combine the cinnamon, almond flour, sugar, ginger and salt. Mix thoroughly to combine.
4. In another mixing bowl, whisk the egg and softened butter together.
5. Pour the egg mixture into the flour mixture and mix until the mixture forms a smooth batter.
6. Use a tablespoon to measure out equal amounts of the mixture and roll into balls.
7. Arrange the balls into the cookie sheet in a single layer.

8. Now, use the flat bottom of a clean glass cup to press each ball into a flat round cookie. Grease the bottom of the cup before using it to press the balls.
9. Place the cookie sheet on the grill and bake until browned. This will take about 20 to 25 minutes.
10. Remove the cookie sheet from the grill and let the shortbreads cool for a few minutes.
11. Serve and enjoy.

Nutrition Facts
Servings: 16

Amount per serving
Calories 152

	% Daily Value*
Total Fat 12.7g	16%
Saturated Fat 4.2g	21%
Cholesterol 27mg	9%
Sodium 124mg	5%
Total Carbohydrate 6.5g	2%
Dietary Fiber 1.7g	6%
Total Sugars 3.2g	
Protein 3.5g	

Nutrition Facts
Servings: 16

Vitamin D 5mcg	25%
Calcium 6mg	0%
Iron 0mg	1%
Potassium 9mg	0%

Printed in Great Britain
by Amazon